BASEBALL HISTORY
for Kids

BASEBALL

HISTORY

for Kids

**America at Bat
from 1900 to Today**

— WITH 19 ACTIVITIES —

RICHARD PANCHYK

CHICAGO
REVIEW
PRESS

Published by Chicago Review Press Incorporated
814 North Franklin Street
Chicago, Illinois 60610
ISBN 978-1-61374-779-7

Library of Congress Cataloging-in-Publication Data
Panchyk, Richard.
  Baseball history for kids : America at bat from 1900 to today with 19 activities / Richard Panchyk. — First edition.
      pages cm
  Includes bibliographical references and index.
  Audience: Age: 9+.
  ISBN 978-1-61374-779-7
  1. Baseball—United States—History—20th century—Juvenile literature. I. Title.
  GV867.5.P36 2016
  796.357—dc23

                                                                                    2015030478

Cover and interior design: Monica Baziuk
Cover photos: Front: Babe Ruth, Honus Wagner, Jackie Robinson comic book, Belle North, Emory "Topper" Rigney, and Wrigley Field, from the Library of Congress; Colts lineup and baseball paraphernalia, author's collection. Back: baseball painting, Library of Congress; Kennedy signing autograph, courtesy of Marty Kutyna; jacket and pin, author's collection.
Printed in the United States of America

5   4   3   2   1

Baseball players are not the only ones lucky enough to have loyal and enthusiastic fans and supporters.

This book is dedicated to C., who is mine.

CONTENTS

★ ★ ★ ★

TIME LINE

★ ★ ★ ★

1845	First baseball club founded
1858	First league of ball clubs formed
1869	First professional baseball team formed
1876	National League founded
1888	"Casey at the Bat" poem written
1901	American League founded
1903	First World Series
1900–19	Dead Ball Era
1913	New York Highlanders change name to New York Yankees
1919	Black Sox scandal
1927	Babe Ruth hits 60 home runs
1933	First All-Star Game
1935	First night game
1936	First players inducted into Baseball Hall of Fame
1941	Joe DiMaggio's 56-game hitting streak Ted Williams hits .406

1942	President Roosevelt says baseball should continue during World War II
1943	All-American Girls Professional Baseball League is organized
1946–56	Bonus rule in effect
1947	Major League Baseball is integrated when Jackie Robinson joins the Dodgers
1951	Giants win pennant over Dodgers with dramatic "Shot Heard 'Round the World" home run
1953	Boston Braves move to Milwaukee
1954	St. Louis Browns relocate to Baltimore and become Orioles
1955	Philadelphia Athletics move to Kansas City
1956	Don Larsen pitches perfect game for Yankees in World Series
1958	Dodgers and Giants move to California

1960   Washington Senators move to Minnesota and become Twins

1961   Roger Maris breaks Ruth's single-season home run record with 61 homers

Expansion: Washington Senators and Los Angeles Angels join the American League

1962   Expansion: New York Mets and Houston Colt .45s join the National League

1963   Second Dead Ball Era begins

1965   Astrodome becomes first indoor major league stadium

1966   Milwaukee Braves move to Atlanta

1968   Kansas City Athletics move to Oakland, California

1969   Expansion: Kansas City Royals and Seattle Pilots join the American League

Divisional playoffs introduced

1970   Seattle Pilots move to Milwaukee and become Brewers

1972   13-day strike disrupts baseball schedule

1973   Designated Hitter Rule introduced in American League

1974   Hank Aaron hits home run number 715 and breaks Babe Ruth's lifetime record

1976   Reserve Clause Era ends and free agency is introduced

1979   Nolan Ryan becomes first player to earn $1 million

1981   Two-month-long strike results in "split season"

1982   Rickey Henderson steals 130 bases

1993   Expansion: Florida Marlins and Colorado Rockies join the National League

1994   Baseball strike ends season on August 12; no World Series for the first time in 90 years

Central Division added to both leagues; playoffs expanded

1995   Montreal Expos move to Washington and become Nationals

1998   Expansion: Arizona Diamondbacks join the National League; Tampa Bay Devil Rays join the American League

Mark McGwire (70) and Sammy Sosa (66) break Roger Maris's single-season home run record

2001   Barry Bonds breaks McGwire's single-season home run record, hitting 73

2008   Instant replay first allowed in Major League Baseball

2014   Instant replay use expanded further

BASEBALL MEMORIES

**"You have to have confidence in yourself.
You're not going anywhere unless you do."**

—STU MILLER

WHEN I was eight years old, I bought my first pack of baseball cards. I was wide-eyed as I sorted through the cards, deeply fascinated by all the different players and uniforms and teams. The one that most caught my eye was the card for Craig Swan. He was a pitcher for one of my hometown teams! I pulled that card out of the pile and made sure to keep it safe.

In the years that followed, I became addicted to baseball. I eagerly devoured stories of the greats of the game, memorized batting averages, and attended as many games as I could. Writing a book about baseball has been a dream come true. I wanted my book to be the kind of book I'd enjoyed as a kid. A book filled with stories of players and memorable moments.

I had an idea: what if I could talk to some former players, to really capture the flavor of the game? But who to interview? Where to start? I thought of my first baseball cards and Craig Swan. With a little research, I was able to con-tact him. He was happy to talk to me, and interviewing my childhood hero was such a thrill that I knew I'd have to keep going.

What began as simply a thought to include some stories wound up becoming one of the most incredible adventures of my life. The stories I heard were so fascinating, I just didn't want to stop. I was hooked. By the time I was done, I'd interviewed more than 500 former major league players and managers, most of them over the age of 80, and nearly 50 of them over the age of 90.

They recalled meeting Babe Ruth, pitching to Ted Williams, and playing with Mickey Mantle. They had witnessed some of the game's most legendary moments and played for baseball's most colorful managers. Their stories infused me with the spirit of the game, and I've included as many anecdotes and quotes as possible within these pages. I hope you will enjoy reading it as much as I enjoyed writing it.

★ **Rusty Staub, drawn by the author, 1985.**

Library of Congress (LC-DIG-ppmsca-18593)

INTRODUCTION

Legend once had it that the first baseball diamond was created by Abner Doubleday in 1839 at Cooperstown, New York, but the man now credited with inventing baseball is Alexander Cartwright. He founded the first professional baseball club, the New York Knickerbockers, in 1845 and laid out the earliest set of rules. In the first baseball game on June 19, 1846, at Elysian Fields in Hoboken, New Jersey, the Knickerbockers were trounced by the New York Nine by a score of 23 to 1. In those days, 21 "aces" (runs) were required to win a game. Some Boston teams played by rules that said you had to score 100 runs to win a game. Those affairs often took several days to complete!

The first league of ball clubs, the National Baseball Association, was organized in 1858 and had 25 teams. The first professional team was the Cincinnati Red Stockings, organized in 1869 by a former cricket player named Harry Wright. The Red Stockings were wildly successful and at one point had a 130-game winning streak. The first attempt at a professional league, the National Association of Professional Baseball Players, was a failure; but shortly thereafter, the National League was formed in 1876 with the help of pitcher A. J. Spalding. Eight teams—the Boston Red Stockings, Chicago White Stockings, Cincinnati Red Legs, Hartford Dark Blues, Louisville Grays, Philadelphia Athletics, Brooklyn Mutuals, and

St. Louis Brown Stockings—played a 70-game schedule.

Between 1882 and 1891, there was a second major league, the American Association. Its teams included the Baltimore Orioles, Brooklyn Grays, Cincinnati Red Stockings, Louisville Colonels, New York Metropolitans, Philadelphia Athletics, Pittsburgh Alleghenys, and St. Louis Brown Stockings. Two of these teams had formerly been in the National League, and others would later wind up in the National League.

The most basic things about the game have remained the same—the pitcher throws a ball, the batter hits it and tries to run the bases and score—but much has changed. Many things about the early game were very different from today. The distance from the mound to home plate was only 45 feet until 1881. Pitchers threw underhanded, and batters could order up their pitches. The distance increased to 50 feet, and then 60 feet, 6 inches in 1893. Early catcher's mitts were so thin that catchers sometimes padded them with a piece of raw steak to soften the sting of the fastball. In 1887, walks counted as hits, and batting averages that year reflected the temporary change. Tip O'Neill of the Browns hit .485! That year, it was four strikes and you're out instead of the usual three. The number of balls required for a walk also changed in those early days—starting out as nine, then eight, then seven, six, five—four balls was finally settled upon in 1889. The number of games played rose from the original 70 to 112, then 126, then 140. Finally in 1904 the schedule ran 154 games, where it would remain for more than 50 years.

In the following chapters, you'll journey through modern baseball history. But first, you'll learn some baseball basics.

★

PLAY BALL!

There's something timeless about baseball—the crack of the bat, the roar of the crowd, the growl of the umpire. Every one of the nearly 20,000 athletes who have played major league baseball started out playing the same way as the rest of us: picking up a bat and ball, and playing. But even though most players learned to play baseball as kids, there were many old-time players who knew nothing of the major leagues or any of its stars. "When I was growing up," remembers Tim Thompson, who was born in 1924, "I didn't even know who Babe Ruth was. I lived in the coal region, and all we did was play ball. Growing up I didn't know anything about professional baseball. We had a taped ball and put nails in our bat. We might have two gloves on both sides of the field. Very few people had gloves. We had rocks for bases."

Many rural areas had no ball fields. This was the case for Johnny Hetki, who was born in Kansas and pitched in the majors starting in 1945: "They ask me, *Where did I play?* We didn't have ball fields like they have today. Guess where we played? Cow pastures. We played in the cow pastures: We stepped out the base paths, and used a piece of cardboard or something for a base. We made our own pitching mound and put our own plate. We had no one coaching us."

But living in the country may not have been a disadvantage. Bob Speake, who was an outfielder for the Cubs and Giants in the 1950s, says, "I had a natural grip holding the bat, because I grew up on a farm and had a hoe in my hands all the time."

Kids growing up in the city had access to ball fields and parks, but sometimes the best place to practice was right at home. "My favorite pastime when I was growing up," says pitcher Dick Hall, a St. Louis native, "was to throw against the front steps. From the sidewalk in front of the house it was about 30 feet away. And I had a strike zone on the steps, and I would make-believe I was pitching to people. And if you'd just tip the top of the step, it'd bounce back and crash into the screen for the front door, but my mother didn't seem to mind that I was wrecking the screen."

★ **Future Chicago Cub Ed Mayer in 1933.** Courtesy of Ed Mayer

SIGNING

THESE DAYS, talented young players are selected by teams in a draft and don't have a say in what team they will play for. Before the draft, there were several ways a kid could wind up with a professional baseball contract. Most were first noticed by a scout, whose job was to seek out new talent. The scouts of old spent their days watching youngsters in a variety of settings—American Legion, Police Athletic League, high school, college, semipro, and even sandlot, playground, and softball games. Scouts couldn't be everywhere at once, so they often had a network of part-time bird dogs working for them.

If you happened to do well when someone was watching, you were in luck. After high school student Fred Van Dusen hit a grand slam and a triple in the New York City Championship game at Ebbets Field in 1955, "so many scouts called that we couldn't have dinner. We had to take the phone off the hook."

A hot prospect would have been chased by 5, 10, or maybe even all 16 teams! How to decide? He might pick the team that offered the most money, or perhaps his hometown team, or maybe the team offering the best chance of advancing to the majors. Jerry Coleman's parents wanted him to take an offer from the Dodgers, but "the Yankees was always my club, the only one I had any interest in," says Coleman, who eventually did sign with the Yanks. "Everybody got mad at me 'cause I wanted to be a Yankee."

Teams held tryout camps around the country that each attracted hundreds of boys. To make money for school clothes, Cloyd Boyer was baling hay in the summer of 1944 when his father convinced him to go to a tryout camp in Carthage, Missouri, where he was signed by the Cardinals.

Some kids, like Hal Schacker, took matters into their own hands. "I asked for a tryout from Casey Stengel," says Schacker. "I wrote him a letter and asked for a tryout. He wrote me back and told me to report at Ebbets Field when they came in, and pitch batting practice. And I did. And that's how I started my career with the Boston Braves."

Owners made personal contact with players and spared no expense to make players feel at home. Dave Ferriss was invited to join the Boston Red Sox twice in 1941 and got to pitch batting practice to them and meet legends such as Ted Williams and Jimmie Foxx. In September 1941, he traveled with the Sox to New York, and Williams took him to Times Square and then on the subway to Yankee Stadium. Browns owner Bill DeWitt called shortstop Al Naples and asked him to meet in

★ Alex George was 16 years old when he signed with the A's on September 16, 1955, and played the same night.

Courtesy of Alex George

3

Boston, where the Browns were playing. Naples did, signed a contract, and was used in a game just days later.

Movie star Bing Crosby, a part owner of the Pirates, used his famous name to get prospects to sign. The 1950s Pirates pitching star Vern Law recalls his experience: "The last people to come in was the Pirates. And when they come in they had a dozen roses and a box of chocolates for my mother. And halfway through the conversation the phone rings, and Babe Herman says, 'Mrs. Law, you'd better answer the phone.' Well, she answers and on the other line is Bing Crosby. Well, my mother like fainted. So that really made an impression."

Money was not even an issue for some. Stan Pawloski, who wound up on the 1955 Indians, recalls, "You're happy to get paid. You know, you come out of the coal mines and someone says they'll pay you to play baseball. You think *Wow, what's going on here, I'd do it for nothing.*"

Many kids were multisport athletes and had to decide which sport to pursue. Some, like Carroll Hardy and Tom Yewcic, played both Major League Baseball and NFL football. Others, like Pirates pitcher Laurin Pepper, picked baseball over football. "Football didn't offer any money in those days, and baseball did," says Pepper. Gene Conley played NBA basketball and Major League Baseball and is the only two-sport player to win championships in both

sports. Leo Posada was one of the top cyclists in Latin America before he chose professional baseball.

LIFE IN THE MINORS

GETTING TO the majors means advancing through the minors, which used to have six levels: D on up to C, B, A, AA, and AAA. Until about 1920, teams purchased contracts of promising players from independent minor league clubs. Rich teams gobbled up the best talent. Then along came former player and manager Branch Rickey, who implemented the "farm system" by buying or affiliating teams with the St. Louis Cardinals, so players on those teams would be off limits to other big league clubs.

Through the 1930s, most clubs only had a handful of farm teams, but those numbers rose in the 1940s. The 1940 Cardinals had 31 teams! The number of low minor league teams was mind-boggling. In 1949, there were 190 D teams in 25 leagues, including the PONY League (Pennsylvania-Ontario-New York) and the Kitty League (Kentucky-Illinois-Tennessee); 106 C teams in 14 leagues; and 84 B teams in 11 leagues. More farm teams meant there was more room for young players. On the other hand, it also meant more competition for a spot in the big leagues. In 1949, Ted Williams advised young pitcher Russ Kemmerer to sign with the Red Sox rather than the Reds or Pirates, because for one thing, the Sox had only eight farm teams. Kemmerer took that advice and wound up in the majors three years later.

Johnny Rutherford, who signed with the Dodgers in 1947, explains: "It was a bad time to try to get anywhere because the Dodgers had about 25 teams in the minor leagues. So there's only two or three players that ever come up to the Dodgers at one time, you know. And it was a struggle."

After peaking in the 1940s and early 1950s, the number of farm teams decreased. By 1953, the Dodgers were down to 16 teams and the Giants were down to 9. The D, C, and B levels were abolished in 1963, leaving only A, AA, and AAA; most teams now have about seven farm teams, including a couple of teams in the Dominican Republic.

Competition among minor leaguers was tremendous. There were always several rising stars at each position. If you pitched for a lousy team, you'd have a terrible record and a poor chance of getting promoted. You had a better chance of making it up to a team with lots of turnover than one with long-term superstars. A catcher signed by the Yankees between the late 1920s and early 1960s had a slim chance of making it because of the dominance of two superstar Yankee catchers, Bill Dickey (1928–1946) and Yogi Berra (1946–1965). Catcher

Gus Triandos, who spent years in the Yankees farm system and hit .368 in 1953 for AA Binghamton, couldn't get a foothold with the Yanks and was traded to the Orioles a year later.

The key to making it to the majors was getting out of the low minors. Though every player hoped to get to the majors, when the time came, it could still be a real surprise. That was the case for George Spencer, who'd signed with the Giants in 1948: "I was with Jersey City, and I had won my first eight games, and [then] I lost four in a row. Joe Becker, who was the manager, called me up—we were on the road—and he said, 'You're going to Philadelphia to pick the big club up tomorrow.' I said, 'Sure.' I said, 'I just lost four games in a row for crying out loud, and they're gonna take me in the big leagues?' I started laughing. He says, 'George, I'm serious, you're going to the big leagues.' I says, 'You've gotta be kidding me.' And he wasn't kidding me, and I did."

Minor league careers have always involved low pay and a lot of moving, travel, cheap motels, and greasy diners. It's a lifestyle better suited for bachelors. Baseball wives have to be patient and ready to move at a moment's notice.

SPRING TRAINING

WHITE Sox president A. G. Spalding was the first to send his team to a southern locale to

ACTIVITY

Be an Advance Scout

MANAGERS AND PLAYERS want to know as much as possible about their upcoming opponents. Advance scouts help make that possible. They attend opponents' games and take detailed notes about various players. Does Johnson have trouble with high fastballs? Does Jackson crush changeups? Pitchers and hitters have also been known to keep their own notes on various opponents.

The next game you watch, take notes on the pitcher for a few innings—his pitch types and speeds—and then switch to taking notes on the batters. Are they prone to taking certain pitches, swinging at certain pitches? How is their timing?

DICK GERNERT, METS ADVANCE SCOUT IN THE 1980S: *"During the season you're on the road all the time. You're one step ahead of the major league club, trying to find out what the other team is doing, what are their weaknesses, who's hurt."*

train for the coming season. The Sox set up camp in Hot Springs, Arkansas, in 1886 so they could bathe in the cleansing hot springs and sweat off excess fat. The idea of going south for training caught on, and teams have been doing it in March ever since. In 1980, 18 clubs trained in Florida, 7 in Arizona, and 1 in California. By 2013, there were 15 teams training in Florida and 15 in Arizona.

Spring training is a proving ground for farm team players invited to train with the parent club. Established big leaguers compete with up-and-comers from the minors for a spot on the roster. There may be 5 catchers, 12 outfielders, a bunch of third basemen, and a whole army of pitchers showing off their stuff.

"You'd have a good year," says 1960s outfielder Len Gabrielson, "and in spring training you'd run out to your position and turn around and there's eight guys standing there that can hit better, throw better, run better."

A good spring doesn't guarantee anything, but a bad spring does: a trip back to the minors—or home. Gary Blaylock, a 1950s pitcher, recalls the stress: "You'd go to this little office they had, and you'd look up your name in alphabetical order. You'd go to your name and sign beside your name, and they'd give you your meal money for that week. But when it got down to cut-down time, near the end of spring training, if you went to that office to get your meal money and there was a red line drawn through your name, that meant you go to the office and get your fare home. Well, I went through two of those. They'd give it out every Thursday then, near the end, so the last day I went to pick up my meal money it looked like somebody spilled blood on that page. There were so many red lines. There were seven red lines above my name and seven red lines below

★ **The Boston Americans at spring training in Hot Springs, 1912.** Library of Congress (LC-DIG-ggbain-11550)

my name. And my heart just jumped up to my mouth, so to speak, 'cause it meant I was coming home. But there my name was. It didn't have a red line. So I grabbed that meal money and I ran."

Still, hundreds of players who never made it to the majors got a taste of major league life in spring training, and for a few weeks they got to play with some of their idols.

In the days before air travel, teams slowly made their way north at the end of spring training, playing games against some of their farm clubs along the way.

WELCOME TO THE BIG LEAGUES

FOR MOST of the season, teams are limited to a 25-man roster, but from September 1 to the end of the season, expanded rosters of up to 40 players are allowed. Because of this rule, many players have their first major league game in September.

Some first games were forgettably bad, others memorably good. Few can top pitcher Pete Richert's first appearance for the Dodgers in April 1962. In relief, the Long Island native struck out seven Reds, including the first six batters he faced. This pitching performance is the record for a first game. Or how about pitcher Jim O'Toole, who found out after his first big league game in 1958 that he'd been

Calculate Batting and Slugging Average

TO CALCULATE BATTING AVERAGE (BA), divide number of hits by the number of at bats (AB). So 100 hits in 300 AB equals a .333 batting average. What would the average be for a player with 139 hits in 534 AB? Divide 139 by 534, and you should get .260.

Slugging average (SA), which measures extra-base hits, is a little trickier. Two players can have identical batting averages of .300, but one might have a .400 SA while another has a .600 SA. To determine slugging average, you must calculate the total bases achieved by a batter. A single is 1, a double 2, a triple 3, and a home run 4. So a player with one of each would have 10 total bases. The number of total bases is divided into the number of AB to calculate the batter's slugging average. A player with 100 singles, 40 doubles, no triples, and no home runs in 300 at bats would have the same slugging percentage as one with 100 singles, no doubles or triples, and 20 home runs in 300 at bats.

What would the batting and slugging averages be for a player with 85 singles, 10 doubles, 5 triples, and 15 home runs in 400 AB? (The answers are below.)

Power hitters achieve .600 or better. Babe Ruth topped .700 nine times and in 1920 had an incredible .847 slugging average, which was topped only by Barry Bonds, who had a .863 SA in 2001.

Another, lesser-used statistic is home run percentage (homers divided into AB, times 100). A player who hits 20 home runs in 500 AB would have a 4.0 percent home run percentage. The lifetime leader in home run percentage is Mark McGwire at 9.4 percent, followed by Babe Ruth at 8.5 percent.

BA = .288 and SA = .450

Calculate ERA

EARNED RUN AVERAGE (ERA) is the most accurate way to measure a pitcher's abilities. ERA shows on average how many runs a pitcher gives up per nine innings (not counting runs scored due to fielding errors). If a pitcher yields nine runs in nine innings, his ERA is 9.00. If he gives up nine runs in one inning, his era is 81.00. And if he gives up no runs in nine innings, his ERA is 0.00. On the other hand, if he gives up an earned run without getting an out, the way 18-year-old Gordie Sundin did in 1956, his ERA will be infinity.

A low ERA also depends on a good bullpen, since a pitcher who's taken out of a game with runners on base is responsible for them. If Jones leaves a 0–0 game with two outs in the bottom of the ninth inning after walking the bases loaded and the reliever gives up a single, the winning run gets charged to Jones. ERA makes no distinction between home runs or singles. A pitcher with a 3.00 ERA may have given up 40 home runs, while a pitcher with a 4.00 ERA may have only given up 10. When Hal Stowe pitched one inning for the 1960 Yankees, he gave up a walk and balked. The runner advanced to third on a sacrifice and scored on a sacrifice fly. No hits but one earned run in one inning left Stowe's ERA for the year as 9.00.

To calculate ERA, divide number of innings pitched by nine. Then take that result and divide it into the number of earned runs given up. For example, consider 38 innings pitched and 47 earned runs.

$$38 \div 9 = 4.22$$
$$47 \div 4.22 = 11.14 \text{ ERA (not very impressive).}$$

See if you can figure out how many runs each of these pitchers gave up:

In 1957, Milt Pappas pitched nine innings and had an ERA of 1.00.

In 1953, Tom Qualters pitched one-third of an inning and had an ERA of 162.00.

In 1923, Bob Potter pitched three innings and had an ERA of 21.00.

Pappas, 1 run; Qualters, 6 runs; Potter, 7 runs

named Minor League Pitcher of the Year and was invited to appear on the *Ed Sullivan Show* alongside Mickey Mantle and Yogi Berra?

Here are some other first game stories:

Eddie Yost, 1944 Senators: "I faced Lee, a left-handed pitcher. The manager put me up to pinch hit, and I took three strikes. I was so damn nervous, I didn't know what town I was in. I struck out. Didn't even swing the bat. I can remember, Bobo Newsom, he was on the bench, 'Swing the bat! Swing the bat!'"

Dick Welteroth, 1948 Senators: "The first game I went into was against the Boston Red Sox, and the first three hitters I pitched against were Williams, Doerr, and Pesky, and I got them out one, two, three. I came back to the dugout after the

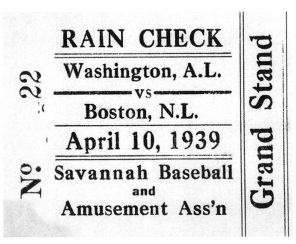

Author's collection

inning and hung my glove up—they had hooks at the back of the dugout—and a couple of the players said, 'What the heck are you doing that for?' I said, 'My day was made.'"

Johnny Logan, 1951 Braves: "My first game, against the New York Giants, in '51. Major leagues, in Boston. Willie Mays was on the team, and Sal Maglie, and all them guys. The Giants! And we won that game. The Boston Braves beat the Giants 2–1. I got a hit, hitting .333. One for three. I fielded about seven chances without [any] errors. And then the conclusion was we won. And I said, 'Boy, I'm up in the major leagues!' Now the second game, I'm hitting eighth. Billy Southworth is the manager. In the second inning, we got bases loaded, and I'm coming up with two outs. Time out. Billy Southworth came over and put his arm around me, and he said, 'Hey kid, I'm taking you out for a pinch hitter.' In the second inning. And I went to the dugout all by myself, sat in the corner, doing a lot of thinking. I said, second inning? After playing triple-A ball for three years, I said to myself, 'Shall I pull for Willard Marshall to get a hit, or should he ground out?' And you know what he did? He grounded out! And I said, 'I could have done that!'"

★ **Letter from a boy to Dodger star Bobby Bragan, 1941.**

October 17, 1941

Dear Bob,

I bet you think its silly of me writing you this letter.

The reason I am writing you this letter is that I would like you to give me some pointers on fielding and hitting.

I also would like you to do me one more favor, it is: would you kindly try and send me a photo of yourself.

Honest Bob, you dont know what a favor you will be doing me.

Hoping you will agree with me, I'll bring my letter to a close.

Sincerely Yours
A Loyal Admirer

The "Triple Crown" is achieved when a batter leads the league in batting average, home runs, and RBIs. It has only happened 16 times, with Ted Williams and Rogers Hornsby each garnering two crowns.

Neal Hertweck, 1952 Cardinals: "In St. Louis, you go from the clubhouse to the dugout, you had to go through an area that was open to the public, and maybe ten steps across the big aisle there, and then you went into a door that went down the steps to the dugout. Ushers would stand there and kind of keep an aisle open for you. So as I was going to the door to get to the dugout, two youngsters were there. 'Sign my card, sign my scorecard, gimme an autograph!' So I said, 'Well, you know, OK, I'm a big-time ballplayer here, I can do that.' So I signed the youngster's scorecard, and just as I opened the door, then I heard the one kid say, 'Well, who'd you get, who'd you get?' And the other kid says, 'Neal Hertweck.' And the other boy says, 'Who in the heck is that?' Your bubble gets burst in a hurry."

Bob Skinner, 1954 Pirates: "Fred Haney called me into his office and said, 'Listen, what I want you to do is just observe for a week. You're not gonna play. Preston Ward will be playing first base.' He said, 'Take it easy, and get your feet on the ground, and we'll go from there.' So I was the most relaxed rookie that ever hit the major leagues. My manager told me I didn't have to worry about playing or anything. Robin Roberts is pitching that day against Bob Friend. As things go in baseball, we were behind 3–1 in the eighth inning, and I hear this voice say, 'Skinner, get a bat!'

Well, I didn't even have a bat. So he sent me up there to pinch hit for Friend, and Robin Roberts just threw a fastball right by. I was so nervous; my legs were shaking and that cocky relaxed rookie was now the most nervous guy in town. I'd never seen 35,000 people before in the stands, and they were all hollering. So anyhow, he threw another pitch, and before I knew it, he had two strikes on me. And I said, *Oh, I gotta do something here.* So he threw the next pitch and, lo and behold, I got a base hit right through the middle, drove in two runs, and tied the game, and we went on to win."

Bobby Henrich, 1957 Reds: "We were playing the Giants in Cincinnati, and my first at bat I hit a ball to right center field and actually thought the thing was going out, in my first major league at bat. And then someone comes leaping up against the fence and drags it down. Turns out it was Willie Mays. And I get back to the dugout and I says, 'God, I thought that was out of here.' And one of the guys at the end of the bench, I forget who it was, says, 'Kid, they catch those up here.'"

MANAGERS

EVERY MANAGER has his own unique quirks, habits, and reputation. Get on your manager's good side, and you'll see lots of action. Get on his bad side, and you'll be benched.

Cubs manager Stan Hack told pitcher Jim Willis one day in 1954, "Today you start. If you lose, you go. If you win, you stay." He lost and left. Scrappy Leo Durocher, famous for his quip "Nice guys finish last," had a fondness for arguing with umpires and gambling on everything from horses to billiards. His scrappy approach to life matched his scrappy approach to baseball. Mike Sandlock, who played for him in 1945, says, "Durocher played the old game. His idea was to play for one run, so the other team had to get two. We used to bunt, hit and run, which you don't see much of today."

Two-time pennant winner Al Lopez once pulled right-fielder Floyd Robinson from a game after he didn't run out a pop-up and told him, "You sit there right next to me. You don't move, you don't say one word. And I'll have a few words with you after the game."

Grumpy Rogers Hornsby had the habit of sitting in the hotel lobby, watching the comings and goings of his players like a hawk. So disliked was Hornsby that after Browns owner Bill Veeck fired him in midseason 1952, the players gave Veeck an engraved trophy as thanks. "Rogers would be way down the end of the dugout, as far as he could get in the dugout," remembers George Lerchen, who played for Hornsby in 1953. "And the rest of the team would be at the other end of the dugout. He would never call any ballplayer by his name."

Managers develop a reputation, and it often sticks with them. That was the case for "mean" Fred Hutchinson, who managed for 12 years. Says Ted Wills: "I don't think he liked anybody. One time a Mets pitcher hit Frank Robinson on the arm. I'm pitching that day, and he yells out at me, 'Wills, if you don't hit that pitcher, it's gonna cost you five hundred dollars!' You should have seen it, it was kind of funny, 'cause the pitcher knew I was gonna throw at him. It's hard to hit somebody when they know you're gonna throw at them."

One of the most fearsome competitors was "Little Napoleon" John McGraw, longtime Giants manager, who led them to 10 pennants and three World Series victories. The fiery manager was ejected 118 times in his career. McGraw once fined a player who'd been given a bunt sign for hitting a home run. His first base coach once said, "McGraw eats gunpowder every morning for breakfast and washes it down with blood."

BILL MONBOUQUETTE:
"I learned a long time ago from Sal Maglie: 'You're not entitled to mistakes. If the other pitcher's not giving up a run, then you can't give up a run.'"

Charlie Lindstrom's father played for McGraw: "In those days, baseball managers were tough. They were unquestioned. They were dictators. And John McGraw was a hardnosed guy. For whatever the reason, my dad had the ability to stand up to McGraw, and nobody else did."

To win, a manager needs a good team. Casey Stengel was very successful with the Yankees—10 pennants and seven World Series championships—but less so with the Boston Bees/Braves and Mets. Stengel employed a platoon system, which alternated left-handed and right-handed players based on the opponent's starting pitcher. Former Met Joe Christopher is thankful to Stengel: "He was the one that saved a lot of players' careers because many players could not play every day. When he created the platoon system, he helped a lot of guys to be in the major leagues a longer time."

There's more to managing than just the game itself. Just ask Joe Altobelli, who managed in the majors for seven years: "I don't think that I only tried to teach them baseball, you know, how to hit or how to play. I think the most important thing a manager does, especially in the minor leagues, is he teaches them how to live."

Some of the most successful managers never played in the majors, including Jim Frey, who won Manager of the Year in 1984, and Jack McKeon, who led the Marlins to a World Series victory in 2003. Walter Alston managed the Dodgers for 3,658 games from 1954 to 1976, yet his entire major league playing career consisted of one at bat for the 1936 Cardinals. (He struck out.)

COACHES

COACHES ARE an important part of any team. First and third base coaches relay signs to the hitters and give direction to baserunners both before and during a play. The pitching coach helps the pitching staff improve, and the hitting coach does the same with batters. A bullpen coach watches and helps relievers as they warm up.

"Sometimes you go out there because you see something that they're doing wrong," says longtime pitching coach Mel Stottlemyre. "Or if they can make a small adjustment during the course of the game. And then other times, you're out there just to take up a little bit of time and give the pitcher in the bullpen who's gonna come in an opportunity to get loose."

A new pitching coach can make a big difference. It did for "Sudden" Sam McDowell on the 1968 White Sox, who says, "Alvin Dark brought Jack Sanford in as a pitching coach. He would sit on the bench with me during the game and explain to me what I should have done, what I shouldn't have done, what I did do that was

OFFICIAL BATTING ORDER

CLUB **ATLANTA**   DATE 7/8/79

	ORIGINAL		CHANGE	ALSO ELIGIBLE
1	Royster 5	B		Chaney
		C		Lum
2	Matthews 9	B		Pocoroba
		C		Bonnell
3	Office 8	B		Benedict
		C		Burroughs
4	Horner 3	B		
		C		
5	Nolan 2	B		
		C		Skok
6	Spikes 7	B	Bonnell	Mahler
		C		B McLaughlin
7	Hubbard 4	B		J McLaughlin
		C		Garber
8	Frias 6	B		Devine
		C		Hanna
9	Matula 1	B		Solomon
		C		Niekro
		D		Brizzdara
		E		

MANAGER'S SIGNATURE......................

★ **ABOVE:** Managers hand in lineup cards to the umpires before each game. This is a Braves lineup from 1979. Author's collection

★ **RIGHT:** Lou Boudreau was player-manager for the Indians during the 1940s. Author's collection

good, and so on according to the science of pitching, and I just built on that."

OWNERS AND SALARIES

HOW OFTEN someone gets to play is up to the manager, but how long he stays and how much he makes is up to the team's owner or general manager (GM). They run the club off the field, managing finances, making trades, and signing new players. They can have a big impact on a team's success. During George Weiss's time as Yankees general manager (1947–1960), the team won 10 pennants and seven World Series.

Some teams have one owner for many years. The Red Sox were owned by Tom Yawkey from 1933 to 1976, and the Senators were owned by Clark Griffith from 1920 to 1955. Several movie stars have been owners. Bing Crosby took an active interest as part owner of the Pirates; his movie costar Bob Hope was part owner of the Indians for many years; and Gene Autry was a well-loved owner of the Angels.

In the days before agents and multiyear contracts, if you wanted a raise, you had to go ask the general manager or owner yourself. When Randy Jackson was traded from the Cubs to the Dodgers, he was told he'd be given $20,000—the same as the year before. He wrote to GM Buzzie Bavasi, explaining that he'd been on the All-Star team in 1955, had hit 21 home runs, and had led the league in putouts and assists. Bavasi's reply was, "You did all that with the Cubs. You didn't do anything with the Dodgers. But you seem like a nice guy. I'll give you a $1,000 raise." Bavasi also gave Chuck Kress, newly acquired from the Tigers in 1954, a raise, from $7,500 to $9,000, after Kress told him that Detroit had promised him a raise. On the other hand, after Bobby Shantz of the Athletics won the 1952 MVP Award, Connie Mack raised his salary from $12,000 to $25,000 without Shantz even asking.

Athletics pitcher Cloyd Boyer had a similar experience, midseason in 1955: "I had a 5-1 record, and I'll never forget this—Lou Boudreau went into the office and got me a $3,000 raise. I guess because I was pitching pretty good at the time and everything. And I didn't win another game the rest of the year. My arm just went dead on me."

After Don Schwall's 15-7 rookie season for the Red Sox in 1961, GM Tom Yawkey called Schwall to his office and handed him a bonus check for $10,000 for his good performance, which seemed like an awful lot of money—$4,000 more than his entire year's salary. "I thought I was a millionaire!" recalls Schwall.

Management can be quirky, which makes salary negotiations interesting. Dodgers pitcher Phil Regan recalls an odd experience with

Buzzie Bavasi: "He asked me what I wanted. I'd talked to [teammate] Perranoski, [and] he told me to ask for 40. So I said, '$40,000.' He said, 'OK, I know what you want now.' He took five little pieces of paper, and he lined them all up. He threw them on the table and said, 'Pick one.' So I picked one out, and it said $37,500. He said, 'Is that fine?' I said, 'Yeah, that's OK.' He said, 'Well, this is my bad day. Look at the rest of them.' The next one was $37,000, then it went down to $36,500, then to $36,000, then $35,000. I had picked the highest one. I don't know how I did it, but I did it. But that's the way he did it. He threw pieces of paper on there and said pick one. I'd have probably signed for any of them."

Good performance doesn't always result in a reward. After winning 21 games in 1960, Cardinals pitcher Ernie Broglio's teammates urged him to ask for a raise. He held out for the first week of spring training, but when the Cardinals said, "This is our final offer," he hurried to Florida, signed, and started playing. It was the same for Bob Addis, who, after a good year with the Cubs in 1952, asked for a raise and was told if he wanted to play he'd better sign his contract.

A player with nothing to lose was the most dangerous holdout. Jim Willis, who'd pitched for the 1953 Cubs, felt like he had other options. "I was making $5,000, and I rebelled on that 'cause I was making more at Shreveport, and I had to take a cut to go to the major leagues," says Willis. "And I just didn't feel like I needed to. I didn't have to because I had a degree in education. I could teach. I had a farm, so I could make a living. So I could bargain with them.... I came down [to my home in Louisiana], they got me, they said come on back we'll give you a $3,500 raise."

The most famous negotiation holdout was when Dodgers pitchers Sandy Koufax and Don Drysdale didn't report to spring training in 1966 after asking for contracts for three years and a combined $1.05 million. After 32 days, they finally signed one-year contracts for $130,000 and $105,000, respectively.

A *good* performance by a *great* player could even result in a salary *cut*! Babe Ruth, who'd made $80,000 in 1931 and hit 41 homers in 1932 (down from his high of 60 home runs in 1927), accepted a salary of $52,000 in 1933 and $35,000 for 1934. Most players would be thrilled to hit 31 home runs and bat .285, but after Mickey Mantle did just that in 1959, the Yankees wanted to cut his salary by $15,000!

A CUP OF COFFEE

SOME MAJOR league careers last 20 years, and some only 20 minutes—known in the game as a "cup of coffee." Nearly 1,000 players had careers consisting of just one big league game, and thousands more appeared in just a few games.

Larry Yount had the smallest sip of coffee. He injured his arm throwing warm-up pitches from the mound on September 15, 1971, and is credited with appearing in one game, though he faced nobody! On the other hand, Gordie Sundin, a top prospect with an injured arm, smelled coffee for an entire year but barely got a taste. He spent 1956 traveling with the Orioles but only appeared in one game.

An injury can get you to the majors—and back to the minors, too. Dick Teed, a catcher in the Dodgers minors since 1947, received the call-up in July 1953 when backup catcher Rube Walker hurt his thumb. Teed caught the first game of a doubleheader for the AA Mobile Bears, and then he headed north to join the Dodgers. While Teed was flying to Brooklyn, the second Bears catcher broke his thumb, so the Bears called up another catcher from B ball. After joining Brooklyn, Teed had one at bat and struck out.

"I was sitting in the bullpen," says Teed, "and talking to some of the players and the pitchers, and we were getting beat—I think 11–3—and I got this call down in the bullpen, 'Come up and pinch hit.' I went up to pinch hit. I didn't even have my bats with me, so Carl Furillo threw me a bat and said, 'Here, use this one, Dick!' . . . That's my only regret about baseball:

that I didn't get a chance to prove that I could play in the big leagues." He remained with the team for two weeks, then had to return to Mobile because their replacement catcher had broken his finger, and he was needed there more than by the Dodgers.

There have been 43 players who barely even got to smell the coffee, let alone taste it. They appeared in a game or two as a pinch runner or defensive replacement but never got a chance to bat. After four seasons in the minors, Fred Marolewski was called up by the Cardinals late in 1953. On September 19, he came into a game at first base in the top of the 12th inning with the game tied 2–2. Marolewski waited on deck with two outs in the bottom of the inning, but the batter struck out, the game was over, and that was the last time Marolewski ever set foot on a major league field.

Some players do well, yet still don't stay. Charlie Lindstrom of the White Sox went 1 for 1 in his only appearance in the majors on September 28, 1958. Lindstrom had a triple and a walk, a run scored, and a run batted in (RBI). He was one of four players ever who hit a triple in their only AB (and the only of the four with both a run scored *and* an RBI).

"The first time I got up, I walked," says Lindstrom. "And then the second time up it was two balls and no strikes, and the catcher, who I think probably knew that this was my first game, said,

'I'd be looking fastball if I were you.' And I said, 'Don't worry, I am!' And I hit the ball off the top of the right center field wall. And to show what sort of fluke it was, I was not known for my speed. So my only hit in the big leagues was a triple. After the game, my mom and dad and I, we went to a steakhouse in downtown Chicago, and we were sort of celebrating. And my mom was really excited. But I said there was gonna be a lot more times to come. But that never happened."

Grant Dunlap, who signed in 1941, got a chance at the majors after service in World War II and time in the minors. He was called up to the Cards in April 1953 at the age of 29. Dunlap was used mainly as a pinch hitter in 16 games between April and July. He went 6 for 17 and had a triple and a home run, yet that was it for him. Same for Cubs outfielder Frank Ernaga, who whacked a home run in his first AB and a triple in his second. Ernaga finished 1957 11 for 35 including three doubles, two triples, and two homers. After eight more AB in '58, his big league career was over. Catcher Gordie Massa got 17 AB for the 1957–'58 Cubs and batted .412, but that was the extent of his career.

Don Lassetter, who had 13 AB for the 1957 Cardinals, sums it up well: "You knew the guys you had to replace, they were hitting 25, 30 home runs, 100 RBIs, so it was gonna be hard to take their place, unless they broke a leg."

Players often wait in vain for that elusive second chance. Roy Hawes was playing for the 1956 Miami Marlins when he was called up to the Phillies. Having played in just three games for the 1951 Senators, he was thrilled; but before he could get to the ballpark, the Phillies signed Elmer Valo, who'd been released by the Athletics the week before, and that was that.

BACK TO THE MINORS

You never know when you might be sent back to the minors. Former Dodger Joe Landrum was called up in the middle of the season when the Dodgers were in first place and were looking for someone to bolster their pitching staff. "You were on a pretty short line there," says Landrum. "You either produce right away, or you were gone again."

"There was a ton of people waiting to take your job," recalls Dodgers pitcher Stan Williams. "I can remember pitching a shutout and saying, *Oh boy, that'll give me another start.* You always had that hanging over your head."

The 1940s and '50s utility player Wally Westlake echoes that sentiment: "Like I tell people, the day they bring you to the major leagues, the front office is always looking for somebody better than you. That's just about the way it is."

In the old days, a club could send you down three times before losing rights to your contract. This rule could actually work against you; if your teammate's options were up and you had one left, guess who was going back to the minors?

ON THE ROAD AGAIN

BASEBALL LIFE is nomadic. Half the games are played in your home stadium, but the other half are played in cities around the country. Before expansion and interleague play, a player would visit the same seven cities several times a year; the Mets' 2015 schedule had them traveling to 18 different cities. Travel was exclusively by bus and train until the 1950s.

Before multiyear contracts and no-trade clauses, most players rented an apartment near their stadium rather than buy a house. After Babe Ruth became a Yankee, his first home was a luxury residential hotel in Manhattan. In the summer of 1961, Yankees Mickey Mantle, Roger Maris, and Bob Cerv shared an apartment in Queens. In the off season, most players returned to their hometown, where they might have a more permanent residence.

On the road, teams stayed in hotels, and players were paired with roommates. White Sox pitchers Turk Lown and Gerry Staley were roommates for years. Lown says, "I was so fortunate to get Gerry as a roommate, because we liked the same things as far as our lifestyle, and liked the same things as far as our lifestyle, and

we liked the same type of foods. It was so easy for us. We were like brothers, almost."

"The average person doesn't have any idea what that life is like," says Bob Stephenson, member of the 1955 Cardinals. "It sounds pretty glamorous, but when you're playing at that time 154 games a year, and you're making 9 or 12 road trips, it gets to the point, at least in my situation, I'd have to almost read the paper every day to see what town I was in, because the restaurants all looked the same, the towns all looked the same. So it's: Go through the ball game, get through about midnight. I would get home, get back to the room about midnight, have a big dinner, go to bed at three o'clock, get up at noon, and repeat it over. At about four o'clock, go back to the ballpark."

Probably the biggest roommate age difference happened on a road trip at the end of the 1955 season when 16-year-old rookie Alex George, the youngest A's player, was paired with the oldest, 39-year-old veteran Enos Slaughter.

INJURIES

THERE DIDN'T used to be a short-term disabled list. Players had to stay out for at least 60 days (reduced to 30 in 1950), and only two players from each team could be on the disabled list. Rather than miss so much time, battered ballplayers took the field while injured. Injuries come at the worst times—just ask Bob Talbot. He received a call-up to the Braves in mid-1957 to replace injured center fielder Bill Bruton— and that very night tore his knee up in a AAA game.

Catchers and pitchers are most likely to be injured by a batted ball. Even with protective gear, catchers have to contend with nasty, bone-fracturing fouls. Pitchers are especially vulnerable to bullet-fast line drives or broken fingers from trying to barehand a ball.

The most infamous batted ball incident happened on May 7, 1957, when pitcher Herb Score was hit in the eye by a Gil Macdougald line drive. The injury ended Score's season. Though his vision wasn't permanently affected, his arm went bad, and he declined from 36-19 his first two years to 19-27 over the six years following his injury. He retired at age 29.

Sliding into second base, barreling into home plate, or running into a fellow outfielder can result in serious injuries. Dodger outfielder Pete Reiser had a running feud with the outfield wall—he collided with it seven times between 1941 and 1947 and was knocked unconscious five times. After a skull fracture in July 1942, his batting average plummeted 71 points. When playing in the army in 1945, he ran into a wooden wall that collapsed, and he rolled 25 feet down a hill behind it. He dislocated his shoulder in the accident.

Chasing foul balls can be particularly dangerous; the sidelines are full of obstacles. Hank Foiles tripped on a tarp in Pittsburgh in 1958 and landed chin first on an iron railing near the dugout. After about 30 stitches and sewed-up gums, he was able to play again in a few days.

You just never know when you might hurt yourself. Evans Killeen remembers a serious injury he suffered with the 1959 Athletics: "It was a freak play. I can close my eyes and see the play. It was a short fly ball to right field. Roger Maris was playing right field for us at the time, before he got traded to the Yankees. Roger had a great arm. The guy tagged up; Roger threw a perfect one-hop to the plate. I think Woodie Held was catching. He flipped his mask, and I, running to back up the play, stepped right on top of it. And I tore my right leg pretty bad. If I would have broken it, it probably would have been a lot better than ripping all those ligaments."

Even just being in the dugout can be dangerous. It was for Cubs pitcher Red Adams in 1946: "I had an unfortunate accident there when I went to the Cubs. Somebody threw a ball wildly into the dugout. I'd just finished throwing batting practice, actually I'd had a pretty good spring there, and the ball hit me in the head and fractured my skull. I'm lucky it didn't kill me, actually."

CALLING IT QUITS

BASEBALL CAREERS don't last forever. Even the greats eventually fade; Babe Ruth hit .181 in his final season. Sometimes clubs release players, but the players often quit before the decision is made for them.

Marriage and family are common reasons for players to retire. "As you have a family, and you have little ones, [when] you have to move two or three and maybe four times a year, that was the hardest part," recalls 1960s pitcher Don Lee.

"My family was growing up," says Dean Stone, whose last year was 1963, "and Baltimore wanted to send me to the minor leagues. I asked them for my release, and they wouldn't release me. They said, 'We might need you.' I said, 'If you don't need me now, you won't need me later. Please give me my release.' And they wouldn't do it, so I quit."

Once off the field, retired players had a wide range of careers. Cy Young winner Jim Lonborg became a dentist. Yankee slugger Bob Cerv managed a hotel and sold cars. Roger Maris ran a beer distributorship. Many popular players, including Mickey Mantle and Joe DiMaggio, opened restaurants.

But what about those players who just didn't want to leave the game? Hundreds wound up as either managers or coaches, including Ty Cobb, Rogers Hornsby, Babe Ruth, Ted Williams, and Honus Wagner. Doc Edwards began as a player in 1958, and 55 years later was still in baseball,

★ **Examining an injured Pete Reiser.** Author's collection

managing a minor league team. Jack McKeon started out as a catcher in the Pirates' farm system in 1949 and spent the next six decades as a scout and manager. Player, coach, and manager Joey Amalfitano celebrated his 60th year in uniform in 2014.

Higher salaries these days give retired players less need to work. Baseball's pension plan also gives players extra money for their retirement, depending on how long they played.

★ Matchbook cover from Joe DiMaggio's California restaurant.

★

THE MODERN ERA BEGINS

1901–1939

The modern era of baseball began with the formation of the American League (AL) in 1901. The eight original AL teams were the Chicago White Sox, Boston Americans (later Red Sox), Detroit Tigers, Philadelphia Athletics, Baltimore Orioles (later New York Yankees), Washington Senators, Cleveland Blues (later Indians), and Milwaukee Brewers (later St. Louis Browns). Now there were two leagues, with eight teams each, and it would remain that way for 60 years. The rivalry between the National League (NL) and American League was bitter in the first two years following the AL's creation.

Library of Congress (LC-DIG-ppmsca-18463)

THE WORLD SERIES

IN 1903, the two leagues signed an agreement. Both would officially be recognized as major leagues. The first World Series was held that year. It was a best-of-nine series between the teams with the highest winning percentage in each league, the "pennant" winners. In 1904, the owner of the NL's Giants boycotted the series, but since then, the World Series has been played every year except 1994. Aside from spring training exhibition games and the All-Star Game, the series was the only time AL teams played NL teams until 1997, when interleague play was introduced.

The World Series packs stadiums with fans and brings in extra money for each team. Players are rewarded for making it to the series. In 1903, the winner's share per player was $1,182. Between 1919 and 1951, the winner's share was generally between $4,000 and $6,000, and the loser's share between $2,000 and $4,000. The winner's share topped the $100,000 mark in 1988, and in 2012 was a whopping $377,000.

WAGNER'S T106

BASEBALL CARDS started out as advertising gimmicks issued by tobacco and confectionary companies as bonuses with their cigarettes or candy. The cards showed a picture of a baseball player on the front and an advertisement or checklist on the reverse.

Eight-time batting champion Honus Wagner, nicknamed the Flying Dutchman, swiped 723 bases in his 21-year career. But Wagner, who later became a coach, is remembered today as much for his baseball card as his career. His 1909 American Tobacco Company card is the most valuable card in existence. Production

★ **1905 World Series at the Polo Grounds.**

was halted at Wagner's request; he refused to authorize inclusion of his card in the American Tobacco Company set, supposedly because he disapproved of his likeness on a product associated with smoking. About 100 cards had already been printed and distributed, so the 1909 T106 (as it's known) is extremely rare. It has sold at auction for as much as $2.8 million.

THE DEAD BALL ERA

FROM ABOUT 1900 to 1920, larger ballparks and the dominance of the spitball and the use of dirty, scuffed-up balls made baseball a pitcher's delight—to the hitter, the ball seemed to be "dead"—hence the term "dead ball era." Between 1901 and 1911, the Red Sox played in a park with a center field fence that was 635 feet from home plate, while the Cubs played in a park with a 560-foot center field mark between 1893 and 1915. The NL's 1902 home run king, "Wee" Tommy Leach, had just six homers; all of them were inside-the-parkers.

Triples were much more common than home runs. John Franklin "Home Run" Baker had more career triples (103) than home runs (93). In 1912, Chief Wilson of the Pirates set the single-season triples record at 36. Even the slowest runners had several triples.

The low point of the dead ball era was the "Black Sox" scandal. In 1921, eight White Sox

★ A reproduction of the famous Honus Wagner card.
Author's collection

players were suspended for life by Commissioner Kenesaw Landis for having thrown the 1919 World Series in exchange for money. One of the eight players was "Shoeless" Joe Jackson, whose .356 lifetime average is the third best ever.

ACTIVITY

Write a Baseball Poem

BASEBALL HAS INSPIRED hundreds of books and movies over the years. There are also a few famous baseball poems, including "Baseball's Sad Lexicon" by Franklin Pierce Adams (1910) and "Casey at the Bat" by Ernest L. Thayer (1888). The former is about a double-play combination on the Cubs and the latter is a story about an invented team. One is short, the other is lengthy. Both are catchy and fun.

Read "Baseball's Sad Lexicon" below. Can you come up with an eight-line rhyming poem about your favorite (or least favorite) team using the same rhyme scheme, A/B/A/B/C/C/C/B?

Baseball's Sad Lexicon
These are the saddest of possible words:
"Tinker to Evers to Chance."
Trio of bear cubs, and fleeter than birds,
Tinker and Evers and Chance.
Ruthlessly pricking our gonfalon bubble,
Making a Giant hit into a double—
Words that are heavy with nothing but trouble:
"Tinker to Evers to Chance."

The outlawing of trick pitches in 1921, more uniform ballpark sizes, and a livelier ball all helped put an end to the dead ball era. Home run numbers began to jump and triple numbers began to fall.

THE BEST PITCHER

THOUGH CY Young (active 1890–1911) had the most wins (511), many consider the best pitcher of the modern era to be Walter Johnson. Over a 21-year career with the Washington Senators (1907–1927), he racked up 417 wins, with 10 seasons of ERA under 2.00. The 12-time strikeout king pitched 110 shutouts, the all-time leader.

You might think such a big star would have a big personality to match, but that wasn't the case. Johnson's daughter Carolyn remembers him as a quiet person. "He just wanted to lead a quiet life. He didn't like the spotlight very much. He realized he had to put up with some of it, and he was gracious about it, but he certainly never sought it out."

BEANBALL KILLS CHAPMAN

"Brushback" pitches were once quite common, and in the days before batting helmets getting hit by a 90 mph fastball was a dangerous

★ **Frank "Home Run" Baker.** Library of Congress (LC-DIG-hec-04684)

Score a Baseball Game

THE BOX SCORE is the official record of a baseball game, but it doesn't tell you the full story. It's only a summary of what happened. It tells you that Jones got a hit but not in what inning. To understand how the game progressed from one batter to the next, you need to keep score.

Scorecards allow you to record a game's action using symbols; later, you can reconstruct the entire game at a glance. If a batter reaches first on a walk, steals second, and then scores on a single, all that can be recorded in a single small square on a scorecard.

Positions are represented by numbers. The pitcher is 1, catcher 2, first baseman 3, second baseman 4, shortstop 5, third baseman 6, left fielder 7, center fielder 8, and right fielder 9. The notation if a batter grounds to the pitcher (1), who throws it to first (3), is 1–3. A number 2 would indicate a pop up to the catcher, while a 9 would indicate a fly out to the center fielder. A typical double play is 5–4–3. A single is represented by a line, representing the path from home plate to first base. If that runner advances later, a dashed line can be used to show where he winds up. BB represents a walk, K a strikeout, and E an error. Everyone has their own unique shorthand to denote certain things, but the basics are the same.

Look at the sample shown here, and try scoring the next baseball game you watch. Put your scorecard aside for a week or two, and then see if you can reconstruct the action.

GIANTS	1	2	3	4	5	6	7	8	9	10	R	H	O	A	E
1 RUCKER, of Center Field	3		4-3		1-3										
2 LUBY, if Second Base	BB		5-3												
4 OTT, Mgr., of Right Field			K		4-3										
3 MEDWICK, of Left Field	4-3			8	3										
5 WEINTRAUB, if First Base	1-3			7											
8 LOMBARDI, c Mancuso Catcher		5-3		4											
10 KERR, if Short Stop		4-3			1 GH										
6 REYES, if Wryes Third Base		2-5			SH 3-4										
14 FELDMAN, p 15 FISCHER, p 22 ALLEN, p 27 ADAMS, p Pitcher		6-3			X-2										

19 SEWARD, p	24 HANSEN p	29 BERRES, c	33 GARDELLA, of
17 VOISELLE, p	20 CEE p	7 JURGES, if	12 HAUSMANN, if
18 PYLE, p	21 BARTLESON p	25 SLOAN of	30 JONNARD, Coach
9 MANCUSO, c	32 BREWER p		31 LUQUE, Coach

Author's collection

proposition. The most tragic instance occurred when Cleveland Indians star infielder Ray Chapman was hit in the head by Yankees pitcher Carl Mays in August 1920 and died.

Guy Morton, son of Chapman's teammate, recalls the aftermath of the tragedy: "They went on to win the World Series. They brought up Joe Sewell from the University of Alabama. He graduated that year; he was at New Orleans. They brought him up to take Ray Chapman's position since they didn't have a shortstop. And of course Joe Sewell later made the Hall of Fame."

Though Chapman was the only pitched-ball fatality in major league history, a close call happened in 1937, when star hitter Mickey Cochrane suffered a career-ending skull fracture after he was struck by a pitch from Yankee Bump Hadley.

COBB AND HORNSBY

THERE ARE many parallels between Ty Cobb and Rogers Hornsby, the game's number-one and number-two lifetime batting leaders. Adjectives you could use to describe Cobb (1905–1928) would also apply to Hornsby (1915–1937): fiery, fierce, feisty, and focused. Cobb batted over .400 twice, Hornsby three times. Both led the league in home runs and every other offensive category at one time or another. Both Cobb (1921–1926) and Hornsby (1925–1937) were also player/managers.

Neither Cobb's .366 nor Hornsby's .358 lifetime batting averages will likely ever be sur-

---

ACTIVITY

Make a Ballpark Snack

CRACKER JACK has been immortalized since 1908 in the seventh inning stretch song. Patented in 1896 by German-born Frederick and Louis Rueckheim, the snack combined popcorn, peanuts, and molasses to create a sweet and crunchy treat. The company was soon making four and a half tons a day. In 1912 the company began putting a small toy in the box, to the delight of kids everywhere.

Almost as soon as the Rueckheims sold their product commercially, people began making their own versions at home.

Adult supervision required.

You Will Need
- ★ 3 packages microwave popcorn (plain, no butter or other flavors)
- ★ ½ cup salted, shelled roasted peanuts
- ★ ½ cup corn syrup
- ★ 1 cup brown sugar
- ★ ½ cup butter
- ★ Large aluminum baking pan (greased)

Preheat oven to 250°F. Pop the corn and set it aside to cool in a bowl. With an adult's help, mix the corn syrup, brown sugar, and butter in a pot over low heat until it begins to boil. Stir for about five minutes. Pour the cooled popcorn into the greased baking pan, spreading it out evenly. Top it with the hot caramel mixture. Add the peanuts and stir everything together. Bake in the oven for 45 minutes, removing and stirring halfway through. Allow to cool, then break apart and serve.

passed. Neither Cobb nor Hornsby was well liked among his teammates and opponents, especially Cobb, who ruthlessly spiked countless infielders sliding into second base. In 1912, Cobb launched himself into the stands and attacked a spectator who had been jeering him. Cobb received a 10-day suspension and was fined $50.

Buddy Lively, son of Cobb's roommate in 1911, speaks of one incident: "[My father and Cobb] were in the dining room in the hotel, and one of his teammates came by and confronted Cobb and challenged him to fight. And Cobb told him, 'Well, you just go on up to the room. Soon as I finish dinner, I'll come up there.' So he did that, and they went up to the room. The first thing Cobb did was take his shoes off. He said Cobb almost killed that guy, 'cause he took his shoes off where he wouldn't slip on the carpet, and this guy was slipping and sliding around, and my dad said Cobb just really worked him over."

PERFECT GAMES

ONLY 23 perfect games (no base runners) have ever been thrown. Cy Young threw the first recorded perfect game in 1904. When Jim Bunning of the Phillies threw a perfect game

★ **Ty Cobb (left) and Joe Jackson (right).**

Develop Your Umpiring Style

EVERY PITCH, EVERY STOLEN BASE, every throw to first base—is all ruled on by umpires. Umpires can affect the outcome of a game, whether on a play at the plate or a strikeout. The first professional umpire was William McLean, who called the first NL game on April 22, 1876, between Boston and Philadelphia. Regular season games feature four umpires; postseason games have had six umpires since 1947.

The record for most games umpired is held by Bill Klem, who called 5,369 games. Bruce Froemming, who holds the record for longest tenure of any umpire, umpired for 37 years, from 1971 to 2007 (5,163 games). Umpires such as Froemming and Dutch Rennert were known for their loud and distinctive strike calls.

The home plate umpire is the busiest member of the umpiring crew. He or she needs to make sure that his or her voice is loud enough so the batter and catcher can hear it, and the umpire needs to gesture boldly enough so that the pitcher, infielders, and any runners on base can see it.

Watch a few games featuring different umpiring crews and come up with your own versions of the following: strike call, ball call, safe stealing call, and out at home plate call.

> **BRUCE FROEMMING, UMPIRE:** *"We have a tracking device, and we have a company that tracks every pitch, and at the end of the day you get a disc. The next day when you come into the ballpark you can look at your score.... And you can then look at the pitches that they think that you missed. You can develop a pattern over so many discs: the pitches you're missing the most are either on the inside, outside, or low, or whatever. And it helps. It's a great training tool."*

against the Mets in 1964, it was only the fifth one in history. There have been 12 perfect games broken up with two outs in the ninth, including Billy Pierce's attempt in 1958, which was ended by a double off the bat of Ed Fitz Gerald. As Pierce recalls, "He was always, in our opinion, a fastball, first-ball hitter. So we threw him a curveball, kind of away, and he hit it to right field, down the right field line, and that was the end of that. But I never hold against anybody for getting a hit, because that's what they're up there for. And I don't think a hitter has anything against a pitcher for striking him out, because that's what he's out there for."

Milt Pappas of the Cubs had two strikes on the 27th Padres batter in September 1972 but walked the batter to end the perfect game. "The pitches were off the plate," recalls home plate umpire Bruce Froemming. "They were balls. And he finally threw ball four."

THE BABE

NOBODY LOOMS larger in baseball legend than Babe Ruth. Born George Herman Ruth in Baltimore in 1895, he was raised in an orphanage. He spent six years as a successful Red Sox pitcher before he was sold to the Yankees, where he became an outfielder and set all kinds of offensive records. He led the league in homers 11 times, walks 11 times, runs 8 times, and slugging 13 times and finished with a .342 average. His 60 home runs in 1927, as part of the powerhouse "Murderers' Row" lineup, was a record for 34 years.

Beloved by fans, Ruth was known for his amiable, larger-than-life personality. And he loved kids, which made him even more popular. Before the 1926 World Series, Ruth signed a ball for a sick 11-year-old boy in New Jersey with the inscription, "I'll knock a homer for you in Wednesday's game." And he did.

"I attended a lot of games," says Julia Ruth Stevens, Babe's daughter. "Mother went almost

★ NO-HITTERS ★

A NO-HITTER COMBINES TALENT AND OLD-FASHIONED GOOD LUCK. Nolan Ryan threw the most no-hitters—seven—between 1973 and 1991, when he was 44 years old. "Every game that you went out, there was a possibility that he was going to throw a no-hitter," says Tom Donohue, who caught Ryan in 1979. "There was always something special about catching him."

In 1952, Virgil Trucks almost became the only pitcher to throw three no-hitters in a season; sandwiched in between two no-hitters that year, he retired 26 batters in a row after giving up a leadoff hit.

"I tried to pitch a no-hit perfect game every time I started," says Jim Maloney, who pitched two no-hitters in the 1960s. "That's the way I stayed in the ball game. When I started the game, I was gonna retire 27 guys. If I get the first hitter, I'm still gonna retire 26 guys, the next guy. If somebody gets a hit off me, then I was gonna pitch a one-hit shutout. You know, go from there. So every game that I threw, I knew exactly where I was."

"Toothpick" Sam Jones of the Cubs had a no-hitter going in May 1955 when he was nearly pulled by manager Stan Hack in the ninth after walking the bases loaded. Hack left Jones in, and he struck out the side, becoming the first African American to toss a no-hitter.

On May 26, 1956, three Cincinnati pitchers combined to throw a no-hitter against the Braves for 9⅔ innings though the score had been 1–0 Milwaukee since the second inning, when a hit batsman was followed by two walks and a sacrifice fly. Meanwhile, Braves starter Ray Crone was holding his own, not allowing a run until the ninth inning. A Hank Aaron triple and a Frank Torre single in the bottom of the 11th gave the Braves the 2–1 victory, with Crone going the distance for the win, scattering seven hits over 11 innings.

The most bizarre no-hitter occurred on April 23, 1964, when Houston's Ken Johnson faced the Reds' Joe Nuxhall. By the seventh inning, Nuxhall had scattered a few hits, and Johnson had a no-hitter going. When Johnson came to the mound in the ninth, the score was still 0–0. The pitcher grounded out, and then Pete Rose tried to bunt for a hit. Johnson grabbed the ball and threw to first, but the throw sailed away, and Rose rounded first and flew into second base. The next batter grounded out but advanced Rose to third base. Vada Pinson grounded to the second baseman, Nellie Fox, who made an error. Rose scored and the Reds led 1–0. The Colt .45s didn't score in the bottom of the ninth. It was a no-hitter, the only nine-inning no-hitter where the pitcher lost the game.

every day, unless she wasn't feeling well, and I always went with her. The games that I went to, I was thrilled when he came up to bat, and I'd always cross my fingers and hope he'd hit a home run. And lots of times he did.... My grandmother, mother's mother, lived with us, and so did her two brothers. And then there was me, and there was Dorothy, when she came to live with us, so we were quite a large family. And he enjoyed it, because he hadn't had much family life, really."

One legendary Ruth moment occurred during the 1932 World Series against the Cubs. After winning the first two games in New York, the Yankees' reception in Chicago was a bit sour. Cubs fans pelted the field with lemons to show their disdain. Facing Cubs pitcher Charlie Root, Ruth homered in the first inning. But by Ruth's turn in the fifth, the score was tied 4–4. The Cubs taunted Ruth. Root threw a called strike. Ruth held up one finger. Another called strike. Ruth held up two fingers. More jeers from the Cubs dugout. What Ruth did next has been the subject of much speculation—by several accounts, he pointed at center field. Some speculated that he was pointing at the pitcher, and others said he was signaling that he had one strike left. In any case, he then proceeded to hit a line drive home run into the

★ **Babe Ruth in 1921.** Library of Congress (LC-DIG-ggbain-32387)

center field bleachers. The Yankees won the game and the series, and the "called shot" became one of baseball's most magical stories.

Even years after the incident, Root denied that Ruth had pointed. Paul Schramka, who played for the Cubs in 1953, when Root was pitching coach, says, "He said that was some reporter's daydream. He said, 'Nobody points on me. If I figured they were pointing, he'd be sitting on his butt in the batter's box, not swinging at the next pitch.'"

Ruth left the Yankees after 1934 and joined the Boston Braves at the age of 40. He played in just 28 games, but he went out with a bang. Ruth hit his last three home runs in one game. At the time he retired from playing in 1935, Ruth's 714 home runs were the most anyone had ever hit, *by hundreds.*

Ruth was first base coach for the Dodgers in 1938, and after that he was not officially involved in Major League Baseball, though he appeared in many charity games and was still part of the baseball world. Bob Usher remembers seeing him in March 1948: "We were training in Tampa, Florida, and he came to our training camp on or about the 14th of March, in a full camelhair coat with a matching cap. He passed away in August the same year. He signed a baseball to me personally. The baseball is my most prized possession. We shook hands, and I thanked him for the ball."

THE ALL-STAR GAME

WHEN CHICAGO hosted an exposition called Century of Progress in 1933, a newspaper editor thought it might be a good idea to include a baseball all-star game, AL versus NL. Baseball executives approved, and Connie Mack and John McGraw were selected to head the teams. Each manager chose 18 players. The first All-Star Game took place in Comiskey Park on July 6, 1933, before a crowd of 47,000. It was won by the American League, 4–2, with the help of a Babe Ruth home run.

The game returned again the next year. Managers selected all-stars until 1947 when fans were given the chance to pick their favorites. In 1958, fan voting was abolished, and players and coaches/managers made the selections until fan voting returned in 1970. Today, fans select starting fielders, and managers and players select pitchers and reserves.

★ MVP ★★★★★★★★★★★★★★★★★★★★★★★★★★★★★★

THE MOST VALUABLE PLAYER (MVP) AWARD was introduced in 1931. The honor was meant to reward the player who made the most outstanding contribution to his team that year. The first winners were Lefty Grove of the Athletics and Frankie Frisch of the Cardinals. Jimmie Foxx was the first to win the award three times. Barry Bonds won the most MVP Awards—seven.

The All-Star Game is meant to showcase as many stars as possible, so players come in and out through the whole game. In the 1934 game, the NL's Carl Hubbell struck out six future Hall of Famers in his three innings of work. The 1949 game was the first to include black play-ers—Jackie Robinson, Roy Campanella, Don Newcombe, and Larry Doby.

Every All-Star Game has its heroes. Gene Conley was one of the heroes of the 1955 con-test. As he recounts: "I had a sore arm. The manager of the Giants, Leo Durocher, was managing the All-Star team. I was down in the bullpen. I didn't figure to pitch. Stupid game went to the 12th inning. And Durocher called down there and said, 'Is Conley all right?' 'Yeah, I'm all right.' Went in the game and darned if I didn't strike out the side in the 12th inning. I went in the dugout, and they gave me a big standing ovation. And I'm sitting in the dugout, and I thought, *Holy mackerel, if I gotta go out there again!* And all of a sudden Musial come over to Hank Aaron—Hank Aaron was sitting next to me—and he said, 'Henry, we don't get paid for these games, do we?' He said, 'Nope.' So he hit a home run, and I was the winning pitcher, and he was the hero.... That's how you do it."

The 1958 contest was the first one in which there were no extra-base hits. The National League was shut down after the second inning, with Billy O'Dell retiring the nine batters he faced and getting the save.

"I was really quite surprised to get in the game," said O'Dell. "I knew in the seventh in-ning that [Stengel] was gonna need a pitcher to pitch the last three innings. Stengel called

★ **American League players, 1937 All-Star Game.**
Library of Congress (LC-DIG-hec-22989)

down and said, 'Tell Billy to get loose.' But everybody thought he was talking about Billy Pierce, the Chicago great pitcher. He got up and began to throw, and the telephone rang again, and he said, 'No, he wants O'Dell.' So it sorta surprised everybody."

Partly to raise extra money for players' pensions, between 1959 and 1962, there were two All-Star Games per year. The NL dominated between 1950 and 1987 with 33 wins to 8 losses, but then the tables turned with the AL racking up a 20-6 record between 1988 and 2014.

THE GASHOUSE GANG

THE SCRAPPY, disheveled, and highly talented 1934 Cardinals were fan favorites in St. Louis. Nicknamed the "Gashouse Gang," the team was led by colorful pitcher Dizzy Dean, his brother Daffy, and shortstop Leo Durocher.

It is said that the term "Gashouse Gang" originated with Durocher when he claimed that the American League looked down on them, saying, "They think we're just a bunch of gashousers," referring to the foul-smelling factories, usually located in poor, industrial neighborhoods, that turned coal into gas for use in lighting and cooking.

In the end, the '34 Cardinals proved their worth to everyone by winning the pennant and defeating the Tigers in the World Series.

NIGHT GAMES

ON MAY 24, 1935, Cincinnati fans streamed into Crosley Field to watch the Reds take on the Phillies under extraordinary circumstances—it was nighttime! Baseball had always been played during the day. When darkness fell, umpires would stop a game.

Night baseball would allow more working fans to attend. President Roosevelt, hundreds of miles away at the White House, threw a switch that sent a signal to a man at the ballpark, who then flicked the switch that lit up the ballpark's 632 lights. Cincinnati won the game, 2–1.

The Reds only played seven night games that year. Other teams took their time installing lights; next came the Dodgers, who played their first evening game at Ebbets Field in 1938. Art Kenney, pitcher with the 1938 Boston Bees, remembers those early days: "One of the early games was in Brooklyn. I was in the bullpen, I almost got into that night game. I would have

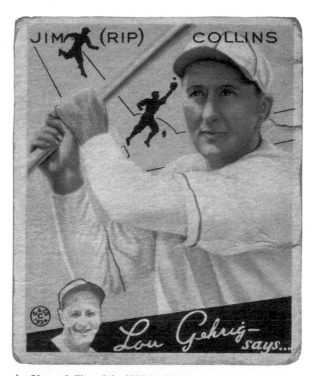

★ **Ripper Collins of the 1934 Cardinals.** Author's collection

★ THE HALL OF FAME ★ ★ ★ ★ ★ ★ ★ ★ ★ ★ ★ ★ ★ ★ ★ ★ ★

THE BASEBALL HALL OF FAME was founded to honor baseball's greatest in the town that was believed to be its birthplace. In 1936, Ty Cobb, Honus Wagner, Babe Ruth, Christy Mathewson, and Walter Johnson were the first elected. As of 2015 there were 310 players, managers, and executives enshrined in the hall.

been in, if something had happened. But we got out of the trouble, and I didn't get into the game."

Four more teams installed lights in 1939, another four in 1940, and one more in 1941. The first Yankees night game was in 1946, Red Sox in 1947, and Tigers in 1948. The Cubs held out until 1988. One of the most famous home runs ever was the walk-off, ninth-inning "Homer in the Gloamin'" hit by the Cubs' Gabby Hartnett at the end of the season in 1938, just before the game was suspended on account of darkness.

THE THIRD MAJOR LEAGUE

CONSIDERED BY many to be a third major league, the Pacific Coast League (PCL) consisted of the Oakland Oaks, Hollywood Stars, Portland Beavers, Los Angeles Angels, Seattle Rainiers, Sacramento Solons, San Francisco Seals, and San Diego Padres. The weather was ideal on much of the West Coast, and the pay was sometimes higher than in the National or American Leagues. Many preferred to play regularly with the PCL than warm a bench in the majors.

The PCL rosters were full of former and future major leaguers. The favorable weather al-lowed PCL teams to play a 188-game schedule, 34 more than major league teams. PCL teams spent a leisurely week or two with each of their opponents on the road.

"It was great because we would go to teams, and it'd be for a whole week," recalls Bob Talbot, who played for the L.A. Angels, "which was good. It would be Monday through Sunday; Monday was always the day off. And like when we played in Portland/Seattle, we'd go up there for two weeks. You know, you could kinda unpack your bags. And then San Francisco and Oakland, they were in it, so you'd go to those two. You'd be there two weeks. So it worked out real well that way."

Joe DiMaggio's career began with the Seals, and Ted Williams spent two seasons with the Padres. Lefty O'Doul, one of the best hitters of all time, spent 23 seasons managing in the PCL.

Between 1952 and 1958, the PCL was given prestigious "open classification" status, which meant it was a step higher than AAA. Because of the great distance between some of the PCL teams, they were the first professional baseball players to travel by plane.

With the relocation of the Dodgers and Giants to the West Coast in 1958 and a new team called the L.A. Angels joining the American League in 1961, the PCL was no longer in the spotlight.

★ **Night baseball, Marshall, Texas, 1939.** Author's collection

*E*arl Averill Sr. led the AL in triples in 1936, finishing his career with 136. Earl Jr. had *zero* triples in his *entire* career. He was 1 of only 11 players since 1900 with 1,000 AB and no triples.

Radio Days

CALLING A BASEBALL GAME on the radio is completely different from calling it on television. On TV, you're summarizing what happens, but on the radio you're actually re-creating it for the listener, so they can imagine it. The best radio broadcasters paint such a vivid picture that you feel like you're in the ballpark.

Try this yourself. All you need is a television and a recording device. Record one inning and watch it with the sound turned off. Pretend you're the radio announcer calling the game. Describe everything that happens on the field as best you can. Remember, your audience can't see what you see. When you're done, play the recording back and see how you did. You can also try your hand at being a television announcer. This time record both the game (with the sound off) and your voice.

THE KNOTHOLE GANG

FOR YEARS, the only way for most people to follow baseball games was in newspapers or on the radio. For many major leaguers who grew up in rural areas, the first big league game they ever attended was as a player. But for those who lived near a ballpark, nothing beat going to the game in person, though many families didn't have the money for tickets. That didn't stop enthusiastic and resourceful kids from trying to get in anyway. Sometimes they were able to peek inside through knotholes in the wooden outfield fences.

When future major leaguer Johnny Logan found out the Yankees were visiting upstate New York to play an exhibition game, "Instead of going to school, I walked and ran for maybe seven miles to the Triplets. I took shortcuts, you know? I think it's seven miles away from Endicott to Johnson City. That's where the Triplets played. I get there, and I go to the entrance, and the gate man told me, 'Where's your ticket?' And I said, 'Ticket? I don't have a ticket. I never knew that you had to pay to see the Triplets.' I went outdoors to the gray fence that had a knothole, and I looked through there to see Joe DiMaggio, number five."

The first official "knothole gang" was established in 1917 by the Cardinals. It offered free admission to a certain number of kids in the outfield bleachers. This idea caught on, and soon other clubs were offering similar promotions. Charlie Maxwell, a Tigers outfielder, recalls: "Back in our day, they had what they called the knothole gang. Back then, they all got

JERRY COLEMAN, BROADCASTER, 1963–2013: *"So I finally get a job with the Yankees, and I said, 'Oh boy, come on, I gotta get three ground balls to the shortstop,' 'cause I was gonna do the first game with [the very famous broadcasters] Mel Allen and Red Barber and Phil Rizzuto; they needed a fourth broadcaster and that's how I got it. So the crazy thing about this was, I said, 'Oh boy, come on, three ground balls to shortstop, get me out of here easy.' This is a true story—12 men went to the plate—I didn't know where I was, what I was doing. I couldn't even keep score. That was my experience breaking into the big leagues. Here I am in the biggest market in the United States. They put me on the air, and I don't even know where I am."*

in free out in left field, in the outfield, every Saturday. So that created a lot of fans, and we used to throw 'em baseballs and do things like that for the kids. Cause the knothole gang gave us future fans, and they would come to our games."

LOU GEHRIG

BABE RUTH may have been in the spotlight in the 1920s and '30s, but all along, his quiet teammate Lou Gehrig was putting together some incredible offensive numbers. "Iron Man" Gehrig's most impressive feat was playing in 2,130 consecutive games. His streak ended in 1939 when he benched himself because he was tired and not hitting well. He soon learned that he suffered from amyotrophic lateral sclerosis—ALS—an incurable, debilitating disease. Babe Ruth's daughter Julia recalls of Gehrig at the time, "When he became so ill, Daddy and Mother visited him a great deal."

Gehrig's Yankee Stadium speech on July 4, 1939, Lou Gehrig Appreciation Day, is one of the best-known speeches in sports history. He began: "Fans, for the past two weeks you have been reading about a bad break. Today, I consider myself the luckiest man on the face of the earth." Gehrig was voted into the Hall of Fame that same year. He died in 1941 at the age of 37.

Author's collection

★

WORLD WAR II and INTEGRATION

THE 1940S

As big stars such as Babe Ruth, Lou Gehrig, and Jimmie Foxx retired in the 1930s and '40s, a new crop of stars debuted. The new stars would become the dominant hitters of the 1940s and '50s: Joe DiMaggio (1936), Ted Williams (1939), and Stan Musial (1941). Each would make a lasting mark: DiMaggio would become forever known for his hitting streak, Musial as one of the greatest sluggers of all time, and Williams as perhaps the best hitter in the history of the game. The 1940s were also marked by two major events: World War II and the integration of the game.

★ **Joe DiMaggio in 1941.**
Library of Congress (LC-DIG-ppmsca-18794)

56

WHEN 26-YEAR-OLD "Jolting Joe" DiMaggio stepped up to the plate on May 15, 1941, against the White Sox, he was batting .306. This might seem great, but not for DiMaggio. He'd batted over .320 for five straight years, with a league-leading .381 in 1939. He went one for four that day, lowering his average to .304, and the Yankees were crushed 13–1. It was a completely unremarkable day, but it was the start of what would become the most amazing run in baseball history.

After the Sox, the Yanks played St. Louis, Detroit, and Boston. DiMaggio kept hitting. Every single game. DiMaggio sizzled the entire month of June and hit safely in all his games. Fans and the press were starting to talk. The "Yankee Clipper," as DiMaggio was known, was fast approaching George Sisler's old AL record of 41 consecutive games, set back in 1922. DiMaggio remained calm, saying, "It's no strain to keep on hitting—it's a strain not to be hitting. That's when your nerves get jumpy."

On June 30 he broke Sisler's record, and a few days later he broke the major league record of 44 that was set in 1897 by "Wee" Willie Keeler. The baseball world was thrilled. By July 17, he was hitting .375 and had a 56-game streak. A crowd of 67,468 in Cleveland's Municipal Stadium that night watched as DiMaggio walked once and hit into a double play in the eighth to end the streak. He'd batted .408 during the streak, a record that many agree is one of the greatest achievements in sports history, a record that may never be broken.

DiMaggio ended the year with a .357 average. He had helped the Yankees win a pennant. His likable personality and all-around skills made him a fan favorite. To the very end of his career, he remained a force to be reckoned with. Bob Ross pitched to DiMaggio in 1950: "He batted one time against me, and I got behind in the count, and I went to 3-2, and I put it right down the middle of the plate, and he hit the screen on the fence in front of the grandstand in left center field, which is about 400 feet away at least. He hit a line drive, and as slow as he was in those days, he made a triple out of it."

.400 OR BUST

FANS BUZZING about Joe DiMaggio's feat soon witnessed another incredible accomplishment. Even when DiMaggio's average peaked at .381 on August 2, he was still behind 22-year-old Ted Williams of the Red Sox, who was on a tear. Williams had already proven himself by hitting .327 and .344 his first two years. But that was nothing compared to what he was about to accomplish.

In an incredible display of consistency, after May 25, 1941, Williams's average went no lower than .393. But as the season's end neared, fans wondered if he would be able to keep it up. It had been 11 years since Billy Terry of the Giants had reached .400. Williams would certainly win the batting crown, but would he be able to stay over the .400 mark? On August 13, he went one for one and reached his season high of .413.

Dave Ferriss, a batting practice pitcher for the '41 Red Sox, witnessed Ted Williams playing on September 7: "I remember Ted Williams... that afternoon at Yankee Stadium had three hits off of Lefty Gomez. Lefty was throwing a 90-something-an-hour fastball, and Ted was popping it. I'll never forget that. I can see those line drives right now."

By the end of the first game of a doubleheader on September 24 (he went 0-3), his average had fallen to .402, and after the second game, in which he went 1-4, it was .401. Two off days followed before the season's last three games; one on the 27th and a doubleheader on the 28th, all against Philadelphia. On the 27th, he went 1-4 again, and his average fell to exactly .400.

On the last day of the season, Joe Cronin offered Williams a chance to sit out and preserve his .400 average. Williams chose to play. Against several pitchers, the "Splendid Splinter" went 4-5 in the first game. The pitcher in the second game was Fred Caligiuri: "I tried to

Ted Williams

Sincerely yours
Ted Williams

pitch him low and change speeds, because no matter how hard you threw, he was going to hit it.... He had two for three in that game. He got those [four] hits in the first game, but those pitchers were bearing down on him. He really earned it. They didn't give him nothing to hit. And I didn't either. I threw everything I had. Connie Mack said, 'Whatever you do, don't let up on this guy.' And we didn't. But he still hit it."

Williams went 2-3 against Caligiuri, bringing his final average up to .406 for the season, a feat that nobody has achieved since! Those who played with or against him testify to his greatness. Pitcher Hal Brown says, "Ted Williams had the greatest eye-hand coordination of any hitter at the time." Pitcher Don Lee remembers facing Williams: "He got in the batter's box; he never took his eyes off you. You felt like you had two holes in you."

STADIUMS

BALLPARK SIZES and dimensions vary greatly. The huge Dodgers' Coliseum (1958–61), a football stadium, could hold 90,000 fans, while the Reds' cozy Crosley Field (1912–1970) could only hold 30,000.

The only consistent thing about ballpark dimensions is that the right and left field lines are much closer than center field, and to take advantage of that, you have to pull the ball by meeting it slightly early; a right-handed batter hooking it toward left field, and a leftie toward right field. An opposite-field hitter will swing slightly late on the ball, so a right-handed batter would hit to right field, and a left-handed batter to left field. Those who consistently hit the ball straightaway will not hit as many home runs because they are aiming toward the deepest part of the ballpark.

Fielders shift their positions for certain hitters, who are so predictable that it's a safe bet they'll hit the ball into "the shift." Ted Williams was notorious for hitting the ball to right field, and managers began to use a shift on him. As one 1950s sportswriter put it: "When Ted Williams comes up to bat, you can rent out the third-base half of the diamond for a lawn party." This didn't prevent Williams from achieving a lifetime .344 average, but more mediocre pull hitters aren't so lucky. A hitter's best bet is to spray the ball all over the field, rendering a shift useless.

When a player is traded, he often has to make adjustments. When Hector Lopez arrived in spacious Yankee Stadium from Kansas City in 1959, Casey Stengel took him aside and said, "Come here son, let me tell you something. You see that big field out there, in left center field? You're not gonna make it. I want you to try to hit the ball to right field."

A's pitcher Bobby Shantz tried to use Yankee Stadium's dimensions to his advantage: "I always liked to pitch at Yankee Stadium, because if you could keep those guys from pulling the ball, you had a good chance of beating them. Down the lines, I think it was only 301 [feet] in left field and 296 down the right field line. So you really had to keep those guys from pulling the ball."

Daryl Spencer liked to pull the ball: "In '53, I went to the Giants as a rookie, and somewhere around early July, I had 17 home runs, and Durocher took me aside. I was a dead pull hitter. And of course that was perfect for the Polo Grounds, and he said, 'Spencer, I want to talk to you. You're doing good, but you're gonna have to start learning to hit the ball to right field in the major leagues.' I look back, and it really hurt me the rest of the year, 'cause I only hit three more home runs. I mean, I hit 20 home runs, which was a record for a rookie infielder, but all of the sudden I quit driving the balls I was pulling. I was trying to hit to right field, and my average went from about .287 down to .240 or something."

The Red Sox's ancient Fenway Park is famous for its "Green Monster"—the 37-foot-high left field wall at a very shallow 310 feet that results in many line drive doubles, and pop fly home runs.

The most strangely shaped baseball field was New York's Polo Grounds, home of the Giants.

Most clubs today have five starting pitchers but in the past, four-man rotations were common and pitchers worked on three days' rest.

This field was infamous for both its short distance down the left (279 feet) and right field (258 feet) foul line, its extremely deep left (447 feet) and right center (440 feet), and its impossible distance of 483 feet to straightaway center. It was a great park for serious pull hitters but bad for everyone else. The center field fence distance was actually changed 19 times between the park's opening in 1911 and its closing in 1963! It wasn't until 1959 that a rule was

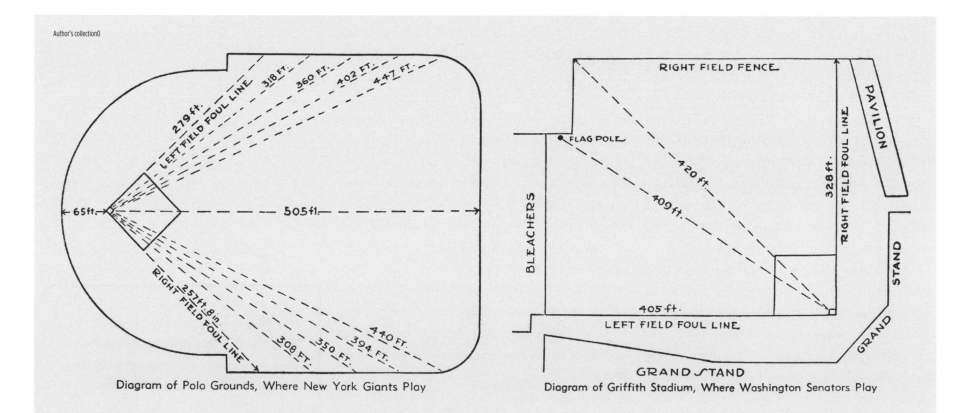

Author's collection0

Diagram of Polo Grounds, Where New York Giants Play

Diagram of Griffith Stadium, Where Washington Senators Play

created that all new parks must be at least 325 feet down the lines and 400 feet to center.

Pirates slugger Frank Thomas hit 35 home runs in 1958 but only 9 of them at home in Forbes Field; with 365 feet to left and 406 to left center, the park's dimensions made hitting homers a challenge for a right-handed pull hitter such as Thomas.

Angelo LiPetri, who pitched against the Dodgers in Los Angeles, jokes, "They had a left field wall that was about 103 feet away. That was the old football stadium, the Los Angeles Coliseum. A left-handed hitter had to hit the ball for a home run about 6,000 feet. A right-handed one hit 103 feet, it would go over this screen that they put up."

Hitters had difficulty tracking the ball in some stadiums—Wrigley Field, for example—and lost it among the sea of white shirts in the bleachers. Weather conditions varied depending on location. The fierce wind at San Francisco's Candlestick Park cost slugger Willie Mays dozens of home runs.

WAR!

WHEN THE United States entered World War II in 1941, nobody was sure what it would mean for baseball. On January 15, 1942, President Roosevelt wrote his "Green Light" letter to the baseball commissioner: "I honestly feel that it

Create a Mini-Ballpark

AS A KID, the author built a miniature version of Ebbets Field using dirt, moss, sticks, and rocks. With a little careful planning, you can make a miniature scale version of your favorite ballpark.

You Will Need
★ Empty, flat patch of dirt
★ 2-inch-wide paintbrush
★ Scissors
★ String
★ Ruler
★ Popsicle sticks
★ Calculator
★ Thick white cardboard
★ Grass seeds or about 10 square feet of turf

Print photos and dimensions of your favorite ballpark. Considering most parks are about 400 feet to center, your scale should probably be 1 foot equals 100 feet.

Use a paint brush to level the ground. Lay out the infield to scale. An infield is a diamond with 90 feet on each side. So if your scale is 1 foot equals 100 feet, the first and third bases would be 10.8 inches from home plate. Make sure you have a 90 degree angle. Use string to extend the foul lines from home plate to the outfield. After calculating the distance in feet and inches to each point, use Popsicle sticks to mark the foul poles, left center, center, and right center.

Use Popsicle sticks stuck into the ground to create the outfield wall. Lay out the pitcher's mound so it is 60 feet, 6 inches from home (7.3 inches). Use half-inch square pieces of cardboard to mark the bases and the pitcher's rubber. For the outfield grass you can plant actual grass. Scatter seeds densely and brush a thin layer of dirt over them and water every day. You can also buy and cut artificial turf or putting green turf. Make your stadium as elaborate as you like. You can even create stands, bleachers, advertising signs, and dugouts using cardboard and a little creativity.

would be best for the country to keep baseball going. There will be fewer people unemployed, and everybody will work longer hours and harder than ever before. And that means that they ought to have a chance for recreation and for taking their minds off their work even more than before."

Though over 500 major leaguers wound up in the service during World War II (including Joe DiMaggio, Ted Williams, Bob Feller, and Stan Musial), baseball continued with the help of "replacement players." Rosters consisted mainly of the very young and very old, such as 43-year-old Indians pitcher Joe Heving. Anyone showing talent who hadn't been drafted yet was quickly grabbed. That's what happened to Eddie Basinski in 1944. Branch Rickey flew up to Buffalo to personally sign the 21-year-old player, who wound up going straight to the Dodgers. Same with Dodgers pitcher Ralph Branca, who joined the team in 1944: "I ended up getting out of high school half a year early and playing minor league ball, and then that was it. I then went to the Dodgers the following year.... It was during the war, and you were either too young or too old or 4F. And that's how you got on the team."

Many who'd signed in the late 1930s or early '40s enlisted or were drafted before they had a chance to play in the majors. Others, like pitching prospect Chris Haughey, had a tantalizing taste of glory before being drafted. On Haughey's 18th birthday, October 3, 1943, the youngster pitched a decent seven innings for the Dodgers against the Reds. Brooklyn decided they wanted him, but so did Uncle Sam. "I received my '44 contract in the same mails that I got my notice of induction. I opened the contract first, then I had the good news. And then I had the bad news that I was inducted. Everybody had to go." Haughey didn't throw a ball for three years. After returning, he spent

★ **Servicemen playing baseball in England, 1943.**
Author's collection

five years in the minors but never made it back to the majors.

Minor league pitcher Lou Brissie had the most dramatic war story. Brissie, who had been signed by the A's before the war, had his leg shattered by a Nazi shell in 1944. "I didn't know whether I would play or not," says Brissie, "but I did talk with the surgeons involved to try to ensure myself I wouldn't lose a leg. And when that happened, then my plan was to go to baseball, and Mr. Mack had written me and told me that my job was to get well, and when I felt I was able, to let him know and he'd see that I got a chance to see if I could play or not."

Brissie went through 23 operations before he was able to play ball again. He finally made the majors in 1947 and stayed for seven years.

WORLD WAR II, FOR KIDS

TEN OF the 20 youngest baseball players ever debuted during World War II, including number one on the list, pitcher Joe Nuxhall, who was 15 years, 10 months, and 10 days old when he saw his first major league action in June 1944. He pitched in relief in one game but didn't make it back to the majors until eight years later. He then had a 15-year career before pitching his final game in 1966!

Carl Scheib, the youngest player in AL history at age 16 years and 8 months, recalled how

'43 National League Schedule

COMPLIMENTS OF THE NEW YORK "GIANTS"

he came to play for the 1943 Athletics: "[Connie Mack] took a chance when I was 15 years old, told me to come down and have a tryout and just throw in the bullpen. So I did that, and he was there down in the bullpen when I threw. That was late in the season, probably September. And then he said: 'You hurry back next year.' That was all he said to me. So after they come back from spring training the next year, I come back and stayed with them."

Rounding out the list of youngest wartime players, who were also 16 when they debuted, were Putsy Caballero (1944) and Rogers McKee (1943). McKee was the youngest pitcher ever to record a win. He pitched a complete game and beat the Pirates 11–3. Other very young players, who were 17, included Erv Palica (1945),

Granny Hamner (1944), Cass Michaels (1943), Charlie Osgood (1944), Art Houtteman (1945), and Eddie Miksis (1944). Surprisingly, most of these youngsters had major league careers after the war ended.

Caballero and Hamner made their debut together with the 1944 Phillies. "Granny Hamner was 17. He'd just signed up," recalls Caballero. "And 'Fat Freddie' Fitzsimmons was our first manager. He was an ex–Brooklyn Dodger pitcher. And when he sent us in, he told us, 'Just go ahead and play ball like we know you're capable of doing.' And you know, he relaxed us and all. And I went in at the age of 16 and played third base."

CROSSTOWN RIVALRIES

Several cities have had two teams—Boston, St. Louis, Chicago, Philadelphia, Los Angeles, and New York. Philadelphia's teams even shared the same stadium from 1938 to 1954, as did St. Louis's teams from 1920 to 1953.

For many years, New York had three teams—the Yankees (AL), the Dodgers (NL), and the Giants (NL), and although the Dodgers and Yankees had a fierce rivalry in their many World Series, the biggest baseball rivalry was between the Dodgers and the Giants, the only same-league, same-town clubs. When Dodger first baseman Dolph Camilli was traded to the Gi-

ants in 1943, the former MVP was so opposed to playing for the crosstown rivals that he actually quit baseball rather than become a Giant! He returned to California to work his cattle ranch.

The 1944 World "Trolley" Series between the St. Louis Cardinals and the Browns was the only one between two same-town teams other than New York. Since both clubs shared Sportsman's Park, the entire Series was played in one location.

Led by Stan Musial, who hit .347, and pitcher Mort Cooper (22-7), the '44 Cardinals had a spectacular season. The team finished with a record of 105–49. The *other* St. Louis team, the perennially bad Browns, won 11 of their last 12 games to beat the Yankees for the AL pennant with an 89-65 record, a huge improvement from five years earlier when they went 43-111. The Cards won, 4 games to 2.

"I was the number-one relief pitcher there in '44," says former Cardinal Freddy Schmidt. "We had Mort Cooper, Harry 'The Cat' Brecheen, and Ted Wilks, and Red Munger, and Max Lanier. And Billy Southworth says, 'Fred, I know you had been a starting pitcher all the time, but,' he says, 'but I'm gonna use you as a relief pitcher.' In those days they didn't use many relief pitchers. If you couldn't go at least eight innings, they shipped you to the minor leagues fast."

AUTOGRAPHS

Besides sentimental value, baseball autographs, depending on age, condition, and rarity, can be worth big money. Balls signed by 19th-century stars can command up to $50,000. Babe Ruth signed many baseballs, but many were played with, lost, or chewed by dogs. Only a fraction survive today, and those can be worth up to $20,000. Babe Ruth's daughter Julia remembers her father as a willing signer, even near the end of his life: "When he was in the final hospital, when he was feeling well, there was always a bunch of kids down on the street, you know, looking up at his window, hoping he might look out, and they told him about it, and he looked out and he waved to them. And he signed little cards, like business cards, with his signature, his autograph, and asked his nurse to please give them to the kids. That was Daddy. He was always thinking about children."

Autograph value increases if a player died young. Lou Gehrig's signature on a ball is worth up to $25,000 and Roberto Clemente up to $12,000. Balls signed by living Hall of Famers can bring anywhere from $25 to $500.

Most fans have an autograph story. Former player Eddie Carnett speaks of his experience attending the 1933 World Series as a teenager: "I couldn't get any of the Giants to sign an autograph for me, but I could get all of Washington

★ PETE GRAY ★★★★★★★★★★★★★★★★★★★★★★★★★★★

THE STAR OF THE MINOR LEAGUE SOUTHERN ASSOCIATION in 1944 was an outfielder named Pete Gray. Playing for the Memphis Chickasaws, a Browns farm team, he tore up the league with a .333 batting average and 68 stolen bases, and he led the league's outfielders in fielding.

But Gray was no ordinary phenom. The Pennsylvania native had only one arm. Though he'd lost his right arm in a childhood accident, Gray wanted to play professional baseball and got off to an amazing start his first year. He hit .381 in 42 games in Class C. It was wartime, and the majors were depleted of talent. Pete Gray's superb performance won him a trip to the Browns in 1945, where he appeared in 77 games and hit .218.

"He could handle pitches," says Red sox pitcher Dave Ferriss, who faced Gray a few times. "You would think that you could throw the fastball and he couldn't handle it with one arm, but he could hit the fastball pretty well. You had to change speeds on him. Fortunately I had good

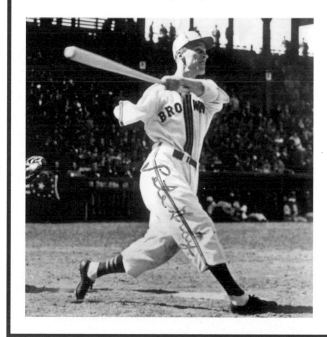

luck with him. He didn't hurt me or anything. He was a marvel in center field, no doubt about that, catching fly balls. In just one movement, he had the ball going back to the infield."

Gray was a special inspiration to injured war veterans. With the return of hundreds of enlisted major leaguers in 1946, Gray's time in the big leagues was over. He played four more years in the minors before calling it quits.

★ **Pete Gray was amazingly efficient at getting balls back to the infield.** Author's collection

to sign autographs. So I saw Hubbell pitch that one game, and after the game, when he comes out, I said, 'Mr. Hubbell, I'd like to have your autograph.' And I said, 'I can't get any autographs of your players.' I said, 'Congratulations on your ball game.' And he said, 'Kid, let me have that scorecard.' And about 20 minutes later he came back. He had every ballplayer in that club sign that scorecard. And I'll tell ya, I hung the moon that night, boy."

Owners such as Branch Rickey encouraged their players to interact with the fans, who were their livelihood. This philosophy has stayed with many of the Golden Era players to this day.

★ **An autographed Stan Musial baseball.**

Chuck Harmon, of the 1954 Reds, explains, "People come up and shake your hand, 'Boy, it's great to shake your hand. Boy, it's a privilege.' And I come right back at 'em, I says, 'Hey, it's a privilege for me to shake *your* hand; shaking my hand is a privilege for you, it's a real privilege for me that people still know who you are or what you are and wanna shake your hand or sign their autograph.'"

WOMEN'S BASEBALL

PHILIP WRIGLEY, owner of the Cubs, organized a new league of professional women's baseball in 1943. These teams helped entertain Chicago-area fans during the war. At first there were just four teams: the Rockford Peaches, South Bend Blue Sox, Racine Belles, and Kenosha Comets, but the All-American Girls Professional Baseball League (AAGPBL) soon grew and drew thousands of cheering fans to games in Michigan, Illinois, Wisconsin, and Indiana. Women players attended charm school and learned hygiene and etiquette alongside their baseball skills.

By 1950, there were 11 teams across the Midwest, including the Fort Wayne Daisies, Grand Rapids Chicks, and Springfield Sallies. Declining attendance in the early 1950s sealed the league's fate though, and by the final season in 1954, there were only five teams left.

ALL-AMERICAN BOYS TEAM

THROUGHOUT THE 1940s and '50s, there were numerous all-star games held for baseball's brightest young stars. The most famous of these was *Esquire* magazine's All-American Boys All-Star Game, played in New York and Chicago. One star high school age boy was picked from each state and divided into teams representing the East and West.

The managers of the 1944 game were Connie Mack (East) and Mel Ott (West), and in 1945 Babe Ruth (East) and Ty Cobb (West). Many scouts attended the game, and several of these All-American boys went on to become major leaguers, including Billy Pierce, Virgil Jester, Richie Ashburn, Curt Simmons, Erv Palica, Bob DiPietro, Herb Plews, and Bud Thomas.

"He called everybody 'kid'—he didn't know our names," says Curt Simmons, star of the 1945 contest, of manager Babe Ruth. "But I remember he said, 'Hey kid, you're pitching.' So I got a base hit when I was pitching, and after I pitched, he said, 'Go play right field.' So I got to play the whole game, and I hit a triple toward the end of the game, and we ended up winning."

Bud Thomas, player on the 1945 West team, bonded with his manager, Ty Cobb. "For some unknown reason, he took to me when I played in that All-Star game. It was during the practices and so on, and he cornered me in the hotel and talked and talked and talked. We corresponded for a long time."

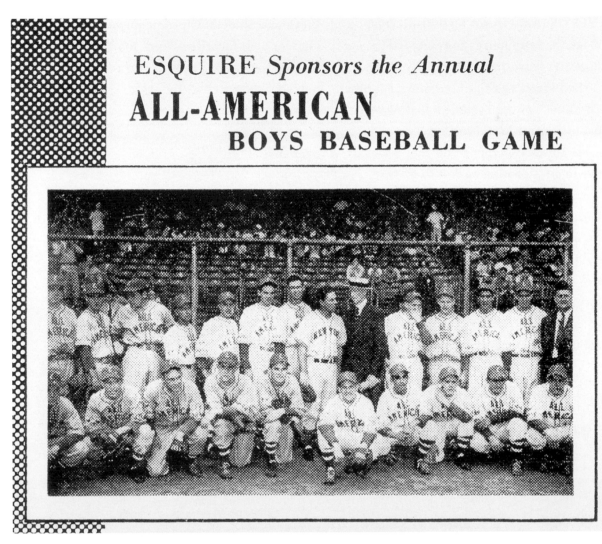

ESQUIRE *Sponsors the Annual*
ALL-AMERICAN
BOYS BASEBALL GAME

★ **Advertisement for the 1945 *Esquire* All-Star Game.**

Design a Team Logo

EVERY TEAM HAS A UNIQUE LOGO, an image that symbolizes the club. For the Cardinals, it's two cardinals perched on a bat. For the Red Sox, it's a pair of red socks. For other teams, such as the Yankees and Dodgers, it's just their name in stylized letters.

For this activity, pretend that a former team is coming back into existence and you need to design its logo. Some possible choices include: Montreal Expos, St. Louis Browns, New York Highlanders, Boston Americans, Boston Beaneaters, Brooklyn Trolley Dodgers, and

Cleveland Spiders. Or, come up with a new logo for your favorite current team. Be sure to design something that fits into a circle with a six-inch diameter.

★ **Child's jacket, circa 1970.**
Author's collection

MR. MACK

CORNELIUS McGILLICUDDY, better known as Connie Mack, played baseball from 1886 to 1896. He was a player/manager for the Pirates from 1894 to 1896, and then in 1901, he became the manager of the Philadelphia Athletics. By 1937, Mack was also sole owner of the A's. His managing career lasted until 1950 when he was 88. Mack holds records that will likely never be broken, including most games managed (7,755), won (3,731), and lost (3,948).

Mack became a Hall of Famer in 1937, 13 years before he even retired. As his winning percentage of .486 indicates, his teams were not always so good. His final year managing, the A's finished last with a 52-102 record. But Mack had a knack for locating talent. He was a pioneer in scouting the minor leagues and colleges.

Connie Mack never wore a uniform in the dugout; he dressed in a suit and a straw hat. In his later years, he lacked the agility of his younger counterparts, but Mack still took an active interest in his club.

"He would put a cushion on the wooden bench in the dugout," says George Yankowski, who played for Mack in 1942, "and he would sit there with a scorecard in his hand and watch the game, and now and then give a signal. And after about six innings or so, he would leave.

He would get up and leave. But the few times I played in a game, he made me sit beside him, which was quite a thrill you know. And he would talk to me, because I was a young kid, about different things about baseball, give me hints. It's very interesting, because usually he didn't do too much talking on the bench at that time. But the few times I got in games, he would make me sit beside him. And he would talk to me between innings."

Johnny Gray, who broke in with the A's in 1954, had an encounter with Mack that he never forgot:

The old Philadelphia Athletics took spring training in West Palm Beach, and that's where my high school was. Sometimes if I could get out of class in time, I would go across and watch them practice.... And when I was coming across [the parking lot] one day from the stadium, I think it was in my senior year [1943], I remember a big black limousine coming up there right in front of me and parking near the front gate. And this big chauffeur gets out of this limousine and opened up the limousine door, and Connie Mack came out of that door, uncurling himself. I still can remember

 **Connie Mack, 1938.** Library of Congress (LC-DIG-hec-24442)

that perfectly, the man getting out of that door and getting up there to walk in. As I started to walk by him, he stopped me, "Hey young fella, are you a baseball player?" I can remember his exact words. And I says, "Yes, sir." And he says, "Well, if you ever decide to play [professional] baseball, you let me know." I says, "Yes, sir." And at that time I wasn't thinking very much about playing Major League Baseball. But anyway, when I was traded to the Athletics [1954], and I was walking down the old Connie Mack Stadium, underneath the stadium there, walking over to the clubhouse, and

who comes down the other way was Connie Mack. And it was fairly dark in there, and he stopped me and grabbed me by the shoulder, and he says, "Hey young fella, I told you, you look like a baseball player!"

INTEGRATION AND SEGREGATION

In 1884, Moses Fleetwood Walker became the first African American to play in the majors, but due to racism, beginning a few years later, an unwritten color line rule was enforced in baseball. While owners were aware of great black players such as Josh Gibson and Satchel Paige, nobody dared try to sign them. They played in what was known as the Negro Leagues, on popular teams such as the Kansas City Monarchs and Homestead Grays and sometimes played in exhibition games against white baseball stars.

Branch Rickey, who had taken over as general manager of the Dodgers in 1942, sensed that the time was right. The participation of so many African American soldiers during World War II and the popularity of the boxer Joe Louis were just a couple of signs that barriers were falling. Rickey's mission was to find the *right* player to break the color barrier, someone who could handle the pressure of facing intense racism. On August 28, 1945, Rickey met with a talented 26-year-old Negro League player from

★ RADAR GUN ★

THESE DAYS, THE SPEED OF EVERY PITCH IS MEASURED INSTANTLY, but it wasn't always so simple. An accurate radar gun was not available until the latter part of the 20th century. Before then, other creative ways were devised to estimate pitch speed. Bob Feller's speed was once measured against a motorcycle racing by at 100 mph as he released the ball.

When 24-year-old Tom Wright debuted with the Red Sox in 1948, he hit the first pitch he saw for a triple, rather than taking a pitch or two. After he scored and returned happily to the dugout, manager Joe McCarthy looked over at him and said, "Son, you don't take much, do you?"

Georgia named Jackie Robinson to discuss a possible minor league contract. During their three-hour meeting, Robinson asked, "Are you looking for a Negro who is afraid to fight back?" Rickey answered that he needed someone "with guts enough *not* to fight back."

Robinson made his debut for the Montreal Royals in 1946. According to Larry Miggins, "I was there playing third base in Jersey City in 1946, and Robinson was there, the first game. I gave him two hits. He bunted on me twice. He hit a home run and a single and two bunt singles. They got him out one time on a ground ball to shortstop. He led the league in hitting, and then he went to the big leagues." Miggins continues with a laugh, "Rookie of the Year, MVP, he beat the Yankees in the World Series, in the Hall of Fame, and all because of those two hits I gave him."

Robinson was called up to the Dodgers in 1947. His major league debut came at Ebbets Field on April 15, 1947, before a crowd that was more than half African Americans. It was a long, emotionally charged season. Pitchers threw at him, and he was subject to jeers and racial slurs from fans and players—even some of his own teammates. But neither Robinson nor the Dodgers backed down, and Robinson played 151 games. He hit .297 and stole 29 bases and helped Brooklyn get to the World Series.

★ **Jackie Robinson.** Author's collection

The door was now opened. Two other teams integrated in 1947. Larry Doby debuted for the Indians on July 5 and Hank Thompson for the Browns on July 17. The Giants would follow suit in 1949, the Braves in 1950, and the White Sox in 1951. The Athletics and Cubs debuted black players in 1953, and the Reds, Cardinals, Pirates, and Senators did so in 1954. The Yankees followed in 1955, the Phillies in 1957, the Tigers in 1958, and the Red Sox in 1959. By 1960, more than 100 black players had appeared in the majors.

Even after integration of the teams, segregation still ruled in the South and teams traveling there had to contend with racism for years. Robinson's teammate Carl Erskine recalls a 1949 exhibition game in Atlanta: "The Ku Klux Klan picketed our hotel, because we had a black player." And even worse, Erskine says, "In the clubhouse before the game, a letter was read by our manager that if Jackie Robinson takes the field today, he'd be shot." Robinson did take the field, and thankfully, nothing bad happened.

Glenn Mickens, Robinson's teammate on the 1953 Dodgers, remembers spring training: "We were taking the bus from Vero Beach going down to Miami, and when I was going down there, there was a car driving beside us—it was Robinson, Campanella, Joe Black, Don Newcombe, Junior Gilliam—all black players. I'm sitting there beside Charlie Dressen on the bus, and I said, 'Charlie, how come those guys aren't on the bus with us?' 'Oh, they can't stay at our hotel; they can't eat where we eat!' I was half in shock. Some of the greatest ballplayers you're ever gonna see, for crying out loud, and because they're black they can't be on our bus? They can't stay with us?"

Segregation was a disruption for everyone. As Jim Proctor, who played on the 1960 Rosebuds in the Texas League, recalls: "Let's say we played in Austin, and we're leaving on a Sunday. We played a Sunday afternoon game; we're going back home. The bus couldn't leave for one and a half hours so that three of us, three blacks on the team, could eat before we hit the road. All the white players would have to sit there and wait, and they didn't like that at all. Then when we got rolling, we would stop and they would eat, and we would stay on the bus."

★ KEEPING UP APPEARANCES ★ ★ ★ ★ ★ ★ ★ ★ ★ ★ ★ ★ ★ ★ ★

THERE USED TO BE STRICT RULES about how baseball players dressed and looked on the field. Facial hair was unheard of for more than 60 years, until things changed in the 1970s. According to 1940s Cardinals outfielder Chuck Diering, "You had to have your pants a certain way. Your shirtsleeves had to be a certain distance. If your undershirt was the wrong length they'd call time and you had to go change your shirt. You couldn't wear any necklaces. You couldn't wear any stuff hanging out of your pockets."

Some minor league teams, like the Chattanooga Lookouts, didn't integrate until 1963. When they arrived at their first road game against the Augusta Yankees in Georgia that April, the team was greeted by a racial slur painted on the right field wall.

ROOKIE OF THE YEAR

THE FIRST Rookie of the Year (ROY) Award, which debuted in 1947 as a single award for the best rookie in all baseball, was given to Jackie Robinson. The next year it went to Alvin Dark of the Boston Braves. In 1949, the award was split into AL and NL winners.

Winning ROY honors doesn't ensure future success. Alvin Dark, who won the 1948 ROY, says, "When I was playing ball I never, ever, ever felt like I had it made. I always felt like, no matter how hard I tried, keep on trying, keep on trying, keep on trying. Work hard. Never stop working hard."

BABE RUTH DIES

IN 1947, the ever-energetic Babe Ruth began to show signs of illness. His daughter Julia Ruth Stevens recalls first learning of her father's illness: "I saw a picture of him and I called mother. I said, 'What on earth is the matter with Daddy? He looks terrible in the picture that I saw in the newspaper.' And she said, 'Nobody knows what's the matter with him, but he has just terrible, terrible headaches.' So they did some kind of an operation, which we hoped would help, but it didn't. And it made his hair fall out, so that it was thin. And then he stopped having the radiation treatments, and they went to Florida, and his hair came back the way it had always been when he was active. And we really thought that he was on the mend, but it turned out not to be true."

Babe Ruth died of cancer on August 16, 1948. The outpouring of love for the legend was incredible. An estimated 100,000 mourners filed past his coffin in the rotunda of Yankee Stadium.

WINTER JOBS

A $5,000 big league salary might have seemed like a lot to a kid earning $150 a month in the minors. As Bert Thiel recalls, "Billy Reed, a second baseman, we played together at Milwaukee, and we went up to the Braves. He was my roommate. We'd talk: 'We're gonna get to the big leagues and make that $5,000 a year. Imagine, make that $5,000 a year. Man we'd be all set.' It's really laughable when I think about it now, the money they played for."

Until the 1970s, players needed off-season jobs in order to support their families. A new

*B*etween 1947 and 1962, the *only* pitcher in the majors to achieve an ERA under 2.00 was Billy Pierce with the '55 White Sox. Between 1963 and 1972, however, pitchers did it 21 times.

BASEBALL CARDS, which were extremely popular with kids by the 1930s, by then were mainly produced by companies (mostly gum and candy manufacturers) such as Goudey, Bowman, Leaf, and Topps. Earlier cards had been offered mainly by tobacco companies. The candy was the bonus; the cards were the real attraction. These miniature player encyclopedias showed year-by-year statistics and various interesting facts.

The golden era of baseball cards was the 1950s. Topps cards in 1952 originally sold in six-packs for a nickel. Now a complete set in mint condition is worth hundreds of thousands. Rookie cards of great players are typically the most valuable. Value is based partly on rarity—practically everyone knows someone whose mother threw out his or her baseball card collection.

Flipping baseball cards was an obsession for many kids over the years. There are a few different ways to flip cards. This version, called "colors," is simple and can be played either for fun or for keeps.

You Will Need
★ A stack of baseball cards from the same year (at least 60 cards for a better game)
★ A friend

Each player should start with the same number of cards, mixed well and held face down in their hand. Player one turns over a card and you both observe the team color on that card. For example, if it's an Oakland A's player, the color is green. Player two flips over a card on top of the first card. If it is the same color (green), player two gets both cards and puts them on the bottom of his or her stack. If not, play continues until someone has a color that matches the previously flipped card, in which case that player gets the entire stack. Printing errors sometimes result in colors that are not quite a match, in which case the objecting player can call "shades!" and players continue stacking cards.

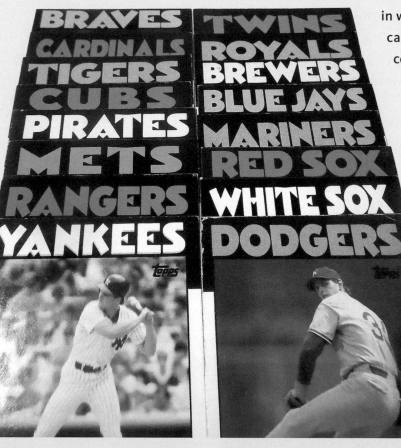

★ **1986 Topps baseball cards.**

Author's collection

four-door station wagon cost $2,000 in 1952, 40 percent of a rookie's minimum annual salary.

Yankee shortstop Phil Rizzuto worked as a salesman in a clothing store. Dodger shortstop Pee Wee Reese worked at an aluminum storm-window business. Jackie Robinson sold appliances. Stan Musial and some of his Cardinal teammates sold Christmas trees out of a parking lot. Ken Aspromonte tried his hand at selling encyclopedias door-to-door, and pitcher Jim Palmer worked at a clothing store pitching suits, not balls.

"All us guys that was playing then, we all had winter jobs," says 1950s slugger Charlie Maxwell. "We didn't depend on baseball for all the money, because we wasn't making that much. And every guy that I'd ever known back then, everybody had a winter job."

In 1959, Reds pitcher Jay Hook, supporting a family and trying to pay for a master's degree, actually suggested he might get a second job *during* the season if he didn't get more than the $7,000 he'd been offered. Hook got his raise.

★

In 1949, Joe DiMaggio became the first player to make $100,000.

THE GOLDEN ERA

THE 1950S

The 1950s was the heart of the Golden Era of baseball. Television allowed millions more people to follow the game and watch the heroes of the day play—Mickey Mantle, Willie Mays, Stan Musial, Hank Aaron, Eddie Mathews, Warren Spahn, Whitey Ford, Billy Pierce, and Ted Williams. Big league baseball finally crossed the Mississippi as two New York teams moved to California, ushering in a new age.

KOREA AND THE DRAFT

OVER 300 major leaguers served in the military during the Korean War (1950–1953), and many more were drafted during the Cold War that followed. Ted Williams, who'd already served in World War II, missed most of the 1952 and '53 seasons while flying 39 combat missions in Korea. Many players in the service during the '50s got to play, especially if they remained stateside at a military base.

"I came up to the Yankees in 1950 with Mickey Mantle," says Art Schult, "and Mickey had osteomyelitis in his leg, and he wouldn't go in the service. And two days after I got to the Yankees, Uncle Sam said, *Well you're going overseas.* They stuck me in a tank and shipped me overseas. The two years I was overseas they won the World Series both years."

THE WHIZ KIDS

KNOWN AS the "Whiz Kids," the 1950 Phillies won the NL pennant thanks to talented young players such as Robin Roberts and Richie Ashburn, but they lost the World Series to the Yankees. Phillies third baseman Putsy Caballero says: "We lost the first game 1–0. Robin Roberts

★ **Williams's return from Korea makes headlines, 1953.**
Author's collection

> **VERN BENSON, 1951 CARDINALS:**
> *"There were runners on second and third and one out, and Musial was the batter, and then they put him on to pitch to me, and I hit a double into right-center, and I came in, Musial put his arm around me and says, 'That's the way to show them who they should have pitched to.' Best compliment I ever got."*

pitched the second game in Philly. Joe DiMaggio hit a home run, I still remember, top of the 10th to beat us 2–1. Then we went to New York, and then they beat us 3–2. And then the last game was 5–3. Was all good games, but we just wasn't scoring any runs at the time."

EDDIE GAEDEL

THERE HAVE been many wacky baseball promotions, but the most outrageous stunts came from Bill Veeck, owner of the Indians and later the Browns. Veeck staged a day for a night

---

★ FUNNY MEN ★

BASEBALL'S HISTORY IS FULL OF COLORFUL CHARACTERS. Manager Casey Stengel was well known for his unique dialect, which was known as "Stengelese." He baffled reporters and amused fans with sayings such as, "There comes a time in every man's life, and I've had plenty of them."

Catcher Yogi Berra was famous for his wacky sayings such as, "When you come to a fork in the road, take it." One day in 1946, Yogi was reading a comic book, and his Newark Bears teammate Bobby Brown, who was in medical school, was studying a textbook. "I was trying to study for a test. I had to take a pathology exam," says Brown. "I had two final exams I had to take when I got back to school, and one was in pathology. And I studied with that textbook mostly all summer when I was at Newark." Yogi finished his Superman comic at the same time Brown closed his textbook, and Yogi said to Brown, "So, how'd yours come out?"

Yogi was very chatty with hitters in the batter's box. One day, outfielder Jim Landis finally

Author's collection

had enough of the gab. "I just stepped out of the box and, not real hard, whacked him on his knee with my bat. I said, 'Shut up!' And my God, he did."

Max Patkin was known as "Baseball's Clown Prince." The rubber-faced comic was a former minor league pitcher who turned to comedy after a navy game where he allowed a home run against Joe DiMaggio, then, on a whim, followed DiMaggio around the bases. In the years after that fateful moment, Patkin served as a coach under Bill Veeck at both Cleveland and St. Louis and made over 4,000 appearances in ball games. Bud Thomas, of the 1951 Browns, says, "He traveled with us. He was the clown. He was funny, he cracked me up. I knew what he was going to say 'cause he performed every day that we played, wherever we were. After he'd put on some kind of act, he'd go up by the grandstand, holler up. He said, 'I don't have to do this for a living, I've got a brother that steals!' I got such a kick out of it."

★ **Eddie Gaedel at bat.** Author's collection

★ DOUBLE NO-NO ★

ALLIE "SUPERCHIEF" REYNOLDS was one of the greatest pitchers of the 1940s and '50s. His fastball was notorious. Even Joe DiMaggio, a fastball hitter, said Reynolds could easily throw a ball by him any time. In 1951, Reynolds threw two no-hitters just two months apart. He had 36 career shutouts and finished with a 182-107 record. "He'd wind up, and the umpire would say strike three, and I'd say, 'Wait a minute, I get three strikes,'" says George Lerchen of the 1952 Tigers. "'Yeah,' he said, 'He's already thrown three.'"

watchman named Joe Early who'd written asking why fans like him didn't get recognition for their loyalty. Another promotion banished Browns manager Zack Taylor to the stands while 1,000 "grandstand managers" decided strategy for the game.

But Veeck's biggest stunt was actually, well, tiny. He secretly signed a three-foot-seven man named Eddie Gaedel to a $100-per-game contract with the Browns.

It was August 19, 1951, the second game of a doubleheader, and Frank Saucier was due up at the plate in the first inning. Saucier was recalled to the dugout, and Gaedel went up to bat instead. Roy Sievers, Saucier's teammate, recalls the moment: "We're all sitting on the bench, and Frank Saucier went up to hit, and Zach Taylor called time and called him back. 'We're putting a pinch hitter in for him.' Boy, was Frank mad. He went into the dugout where we were at and broke his bat and hollered, and all of a sudden here comes [Gaedel] walking out."

Browns pitcher Ned Garver, who pitched the first game of the doubleheader, remembers it this way: "Before the second game started, he had a tractor drag out a farm wagon with like a cake, a big cake on there.... People thought there was gonna be probably a scantily clad girl get out of that. But that wasn't what happened. When they got up there close to the dugout, then [Gaedel] got out of that container, and he went down to the dugout, and people thought that was the story. But then when the game started, and we played a substitute guy in center field and hit him first. And then we came to bat. We took that substitute center fielder out, and put [Gaedel] up to bat. I was in the clubhouse. I had just taken my shower from having pitched the first game. So I didn't see the whole shebang, but I was listening to it on the radio, and I went down there quick as I could get my uniform on. And the boys told me all about it."

It was a comical sight as the 65-pound Gaedel, dressed in a uniform bearing the number "1/8," crouched in his batting stance. Gaedel had strict instructions not to swing at any pitches. Veeck even told Gaedel he'd placed a sharpshooter in the stands in case Gaedel swung.

Veeck believed it would be impossible to strike out Gaedel, since the strike zone extends from the uniform letters down to the knees, which on Gaedel was a tiny target. He walked on four straight pitches and was taken out for a pinch runner.

GARVER'S FEAT

THE 1951 Browns had a 52-102 record and finished 46 games out of first place. It was a terrible year, but incredibly, starting pitcher Ned Garver finished the season with 20 wins, which

Gaedel wasn't the first little person used in a baseball game. In a high school tournament in Payette, Idaho, circa 1947, future Cy Young–winner Vern Law faced a little person in the ninth inning of a 1–0 game . . . and struck him out by having the catcher put his glove on the ground.

accounted for 39 percent of the team's victories. It was the only time a pitcher has ever won 20 games for a team that lost 100. His 3.73 ERA was not even as good as his 1950 ERA of 3.39, when he was 13-18. To further illustrate how incredible his feat was, the other four Browns starters in '51 had a *total* of 18 wins between them.

How did Garver do it? "If they don't score runs for you, you can't win," he says. "The year before, in 1950, I had the second lowest earned run average in the whole league, and yet I only won 13 games and lost 18. So many times we never scored. We didn't get enough runs. And so the next year, 1951, for crying out loud, they got runs for me like about every time out. And so I won some games in 1951 that I had no business winning, where in 1950, I lost a lot of games that I should have won."

Golden Era Memories

YOU PROBABLY HAVE many friends, neighbors, or relatives who have fond memories of the Golden Era of baseball. Interview several baseball fans you know. Ask them about their favorite team as a kid, whether they attended any ball games, and what they remember about some of the big baseball moments covered in this book. Write down their name, age, and other biographical information, along with your questions and their answers, and create a scrapbook of Golden Era baseball memories. You may even want to try to write to a 1950s or '60s player; many of them will actually reply and answer your questions! Always remember to include a self-addressed stamped envelope with your letter and be patient.

THE SHOT HEARD 'ROUND THE WORLD

IN THE summer of 1951, the Dodgers ruled. Their crosstown rivals, the Giants, were seemingly out of contention, 13½ games behind. But the Dodgers lost steam, while the Giants went on a late season 39-8 tear, including a 16-game winning streak.

Braves outfielder Bob Addis recalls contributing to one Dodgers loss: "There was a game we played, the last series with them right toward the end of the season, and I was on third base. And Tommy Holmes was coaching and told me make sure the ball went through the infield before I went home. And of course I did not obey those instructions. I don't know why, but the ball was hit to Jackie Robinson, and I took off. And I was called safe at home plate, and that beat the Dodgers."

A 14th inning homer by Jackie Robinson on the last day of the season kept the Dodgers tied for first place. There would be a best-of-three playoff to decide the pennant.

The Giants won game one by a score of 3–1 on home runs by Bobby Thomson and Monte Irvin. The Dodgers came roaring back in game two, clobbering the Giants 10–0. It would all come down to game three. New York was abuzz with anticipation.

It was a nail-biter for Giants fans at the Polo Grounds in the bottom of the ninth with the Dodgers leading 4–1. Two singles were followed by a pop out. Only two outs left before the Giants were eliminated! Whitey Lockman doubled, scoring one run. It was now 4–2. Dodgers manager Charlie Dressen called in Ralph Branca to pitch to Bobby Thomson. With Willie Mays on deck, Dressen decided to pitch to Thomson. Thomson took the first pitch, high and inside, but swung at the second pitch, also high and inside, and the ball sailed down the line and into the left field stands. Giant George Spencer recalls: "As soon as the ball was hit, there was a *little bit* of excitement that went on in that dugout and at home plate."

The Dodgers were stunned. Wayne Terwilliger recounts: "I fell off the bat trunk in the dugout when he hit that home run. I was sitting on the bat trunk in the left corner of the dugout, and he hit it, and I leaned over. I didn't think it was going to go out. It was a low line drive. I saw Pafko go back to the fence and look up, and I fell off the bench literally on my knees, and the ball just disappeared. And that was that."

Radio announcer Russ Hodges's excited call became one of the most replayed clips ever: "The Giants win the pennant! The Giants win the pennant! The Giants win the pennant! The Giants win the pennant!" The Shot Heard 'Round the World, as it was dubbed in the newspaper, lives on as the most dramatic moment in baseball history. The Giants won the

Author's collection

pennant—but went on to lose the World Series to the Yankees.

DROPO'S STREAK

AFTER WALT "Moose" Dropo was voted 1950 AL Rookie of the Year, he soon accomplished another feat that got him into the record books.

As of July 13, 1952, Dropo was having an average season. Then, July 14, against the Yankees, Dropo went 5-5. The next day, against the Senators, Dropo went 4-4 in the first game of a doubleheader. In the second game, Dropo faced starting pitcher Bob Porterfield in the first inning and tripled. Just like that, he had 10 consecutive hits, tying the NL record. In the third inning, Dropo singled for consecutive hit number 11. In the top of the fifth, after retiring the first batter, reliever Lou Sleater faced Dropo, who doubled to left field for consecutive hit number 12. Dropo had just tied the mark set by Boston's Pinky Higgins in 1938. Sleater next faced Dropo in the top of the seventh, but Dropo popped out.

"He was hitting line drives all over the place, off of everybody," says Sleater. "It was hard to get him out. He was hitting pretty hot there."

In the ninth, Dropo got another hit and raised his average from .265 to .296 in just 48 hours!

★ **Walt Dropo.** Author's collection

Throw a Palmball

ONE OF BASEBALL'S RARER PITCHES, the palmball—an off-speed pitch also known as the four-finger changeup—was most notably used by Jim Konstanty of the pennant-winning 1950 Phillies. Konstanty had been an uneven performer during the 1940s, until he developed the deceptive pitch. In 1950, Konstanty won 16 games and had 22 saves. His palmball was a big reason for the success, which helped the Phillies win the pennant.

To throw a palmball, hug the ball with your hand, wrapping your fingers around the ball. Place your four fingers on top and thumb on the bottom. Note the difference between this grip and a fastball, in which you only use your thumb and two fingers. While the ball is in your glove and you are preparing to throw, pretend it is going to be a normal pitch, then at the last minute send the ball off with a shove motion, similar to how you would throw a shot put. If successful, the ball fools a hitter into swinging too early.

BOB KELLY, PITCHER: *"The first time I faced Ted [Williams], he hadn't seen my palmball before, and he got a base hit off me. It was a ball that he beat right down into the ground, and it bounced over my head and died in between the mound and second base. He got a single out of it. I had fooled him badly with the palmball. The next time he came up, I was facing the hitter that preceded him in the lineup. I always say when you're in a room somehow you feel that somebody is staring at you, you feel a presence about you. And I was getting the sign on the mound, and I felt that, and I looked over and there Ted was, kneeling in that batter's circle, just staring at me, picking up anything he could. And sure enough, the next time he came up into the box and I threw him that palmball, he took a couple of steps in that batter's box and served that thing down the left field line like he knew it was coming and trotted into second base with a double."*

27 KS

ON MAY 13, 1952, pitcher Ron Necciai of the Class D Bristol Twins achieved something that had never been done in professional baseball and still hasn't been duplicated to this day: he struck out 27 batters in a single game. It was a no-hitter, and if not for a walk and an error, would have been a perfect game, too.

"I didn't realize it until after it was over, in the locker room where we were showering," says Necciai. "George Detore, the manager, and Harry Dunlop, the catcher, they came up to me and said, 'Do you realize what you did?' I said, 'No, I wasn't paying attention, why?' And they said, 'You struck out 27.'"

In Necciai's next start, he struck out 24 batters. Less than three months later, Necciai was called up to the Pirates.

ARRRGH! BAD PIRATES!

AFTER GROUNDBREAKING success with the Dodgers, Branch Rickey took charge in Pittsburgh in 1950. Rickey signed many talented youngsters to the club for big bonuses. Seven of the 10 youngest NL players in 1952 were Pirates. Unfortunately, all this inexperience was overwhelming. As early as May 28, the Pirates were 7-32, 21½ games behind. They were so consistently terrible that by August 6, they'd been eliminated from the pennant race! Their longest winning streak was just two games. They wound up in last place with a dismal 42-112 record, which makes them one of the worst teams of all time.

The four rookie Pirates pitchers, ages 24, 20, 20, and 18, had a combined record of 3-27. Twenty-year-old first baseman Tony Bartirome hit .220 and the 19-year-old outfielder Bobby Del Greco .217.

According to Bartirome, "Branch Rickey was the general manager, and he wanted a youth movement. He had this phrase: 'Out of quantity, there's quality.' And he signed a lot of young players, and he proved right, because in 1960, we won the World Series."

THE MICK

Blond-haired Mickey Mantle was the quintessential all-American boy. He was the heir to the spot Babe Ruth had occupied in the public imagination. Born in rural Oklahoma, Mantle tore up the minors in 1950, hitting .383 with 26 homers. He started off as a shortstop but was converted to an outfielder when he got to the Yankees in 1951.

The Yankees' #7 had a friendly demeanor, natural charm, good looks, and incredible power. On the field he was extremely versatile. A switch hitter, he also possessed that rare

Author's collection

combination of power and speed and swiped 153 bases in his career. It didn't hurt that his team won 12 pennants during his 18 years with the Yankees. While Ted Williams was an equally powerful slugger, Williams was not fan- or press-friendly, and his Red Sox could not compete with the Yankees. The Red Sox won just one pennant during his 19-year career.

Just how strong was Mantle? Ask pitcher Ray Herbert: "He hit one home run at Yankee Stadium on a Saturday afternoon. I was with Kansas City, and I think it was either his first at bat or second at bat. He fouled off four or five pitches and it was 3-2, and he took a half swing at it and threw the bat down and was swearing as he was going to first base, like he didn't hit the ball. But the only problem, it ended up in the center field bleachers at Yankee Stadium. Next day, I talked to Mickey, I said, 'Boy you really got it.' He said, 'Ray, I didn't even hit that ball good. I thought I popped it up.'"

Not only was Mickey loved by fans but he was also loved by his teammates. "Mickey Mantle was the glue that held us together," says Doc Edwards, Mantle's teammate in 1965. "Mickey was on the bench, it felt like everything in the world was OK because Mickey was there. Superman was there."

Longtime Yankee infielder Bobby Richardson tells this story: "In '62 I led the American League in hits, and Mickey Mantle had had a year where he'd missed a number of games, and on the last day of the season, he hit his 30th home run. That kept that string going of 30 home runs. And when the voting was for the Most Valuable Player in the American League, the biggest honor I had was Mickey Mantle said, 'I won the award, but Bobby should have won it.' And to me that was just as good if not better than winning the award itself, because he was the icon that played during my career that I felt was the best player in all of Major League Baseball."

TAPE-MEASURE HOMERS

It wasn't until the 1950s that measurement of long home runs was attempted. The first and most famous tape-measure home run occurred on April 17, 1953, as the Yankees were visiting Washington's Griffith Stadium. Mickey Mantle hit a towering fly ball that soared completely out of the park and wound up in some bushes in the yard of 434 Oakdale Street, several houses away from the ballpark. The ball was recovered by a 14-year-old boy who quickly scrambled out of his seat to find it. At 565 feet, this home run was listed as the longest ever hit in a regular season game.

Pitcher Lou Sleater was in the Senators dugout when it happened. "I was sitting on the bench right next to Bucky Harris, who was the Senators' manager. When Mantle hit it, it looked like the ball went up, straight up, and then it started going toward the outfield. It just kept carrying out and carrying out. It was like an unbelievable thing. There was a National Beer sign out there at the time, and it just nicked that sign going out, and so Red Patterson, who was the traveling secretary for the Yankees, he went and got a tape measure and tried to get the measurement. He said that's the first tape measure; he named it right then and there."

The distance of "measured" home runs is often disputed, especially when "projected" distance is calculated. In September 1953, Mantle hit a shot that broke a seat in the left field upper deck. The actual distance to the seat was 420 feet, but if the ball had been able to travel un-impeded, it *would have* gone 630 feet.

Coincidentally, that same year in the minors, another incredibly long home run was hit by Neill Sheridan, an outfielder for the Sacramento Solons. Eyewitnesses the night of July 8, 1953, saw the ball Sheridan hit fly high over the left center field fence and knew it was a monstrous shot. It was later measured to be 613.8 feet. It is believed to be the longest home run *ever* hit in professional baseball.

Sheridan recalls how the distance was measured: "[A man] brought [the ball] over to the ballpark the next day. He knocked on the clubhouse door, asked for me. He said, 'Here's a baseball, it went through the rear window of my car. I'd like to give it to you.' Anyway, I asked him where he lived and so forth, and it got to be passed around, and I guess the sportswriters got a hold of it, and they thought they'd better measure it and see what the deal was."

STEALING SIGNS

MANAGERS AND coaches are constantly relaying information to players using hand signs to green-light a steal or a hit-and-run play. Sign stealing has been going on for as long as there have been signs. Accusations of sign stealing even tainted Bobby Thomson's shot in the 1951 playoffs against the Dodgers.

Preventing sign stealing is tricky. Pitchers and catchers are constantly trying to confuse their opponents. "We had a sign," says 1940s and '50s pitching star Ned Garver, "if I moved

★ **Neill Sheridan (center) hit the longest home run ever measured.** Author's collection

*I*n 1953, Cubs rookie Paul Schramka wore number 14 on opening day. Thirty years later, the Cubs retired the number in honor of the illustrious 1953 rookie who wore it. But it wasn't *that* rookie, it was Ernie Banks, who'd debuted in September wearing number 14. Schramka only appeared in two games in April and then was sent to the minors, never to return. Banks, the other number-14 Cub that year, became known as "Mr. Cub" and went on to play 19 years, with 2,583 hits. "Banks was glad he got it, 'cause I left all the hits in it," jokes Schramka of his former number.

my glove into a certain position that meant that I want that sign, but no matter how many times I shake my head, I still want that sign. And the only reason I'm shaking my head is to try to confuse the hitter, to make him think."

When the Tigers were in Chicago in the summer of 1956, they discovered the White Sox had someone behind the scoreboard spying on opposing teams' catchers and relaying signs back to the hitters. To combat this thievery, the Tigers pretended to make a bunch of calls from the bullpen. They wanted to make the Sox think they were relaying signs to the dugout. Besides that, Detroit hurler Virgil Trucks actually gave the signs to the catcher, Red Wilson, who was flashing bogus signs. The Sox eventually figured out that Wilson's signs did not match the pitches being thrown and were able to adjust by stealing signs from the pitcher instead.

Stealing signs doesn't guarantee anything. When the Cubs played the Phillies in a game in the late 1950s, they had all of Robin Roberts's signs but still lost the game 1–0. Former Cubs catcher Cal Neeman says, "I think it actually hurts. You think, *Uh-oh, this is gonna be a curve ball, oh, yeah, that's right, it is,* bang, and then you wind up swinging at a ball a little bit off the plate, ground out. I think it causes people to swing at bad pitches. *Well, that's a fastball, boom, oh that's right,* bang, and you swing, and it's too high, and pop it up."

THE O'BRIEN TWINS

OVER 350 sets of brothers, including 9 sets of twins, played Major League Baseball. Of those, only three were teammates. Ozzie Canseco and his twin, Jose, played one season together for the A's in 1990, and Joe and Red Shannon played one game together for the 1915 Braves.

The most well-known twin teammates were Johnny and Eddie O'Brien. Signed by the Pirates in early 1953, they reported immediately to spring training and both debuted with the Pirates that April.

"I was always a center fielder," says Eddie, "and played center field every game I played at Seattle University. And John was usually a shortstop or a third baseman, and Branch Rickey had the idea of a twins double-play combination, so they made a shortstop out of me and John moved over to second base. They found out I had a stronger arm, and John made the pivot better, so that was it. It wasn't anything other than that. It was Rickey's idea. I think he was trying to get something out of twins playing on the same team. In fact, to this day there's only been four sets of brothers that played short and second base in the major leagues."

Between 1953 and 1958, Johnny played 283 games for the Pirates. He mostly played at second base. Eddie, who was mostly a shortstop or an outfielder, played 231 games for the club during the same years Johnny played for the Pirates.

BATTING STANCES

EVERY HITTER has a unique batting stance. Many look very similar to one another, but a few batters throughout baseball history have stood out. One of the most distinct was Stan Lopata, who changed his stance in 1954 to a deep crouch after Rogers Hornsby told Lopata he needed to try to get a piece of every ball he swung at.

"I had a friend in the minors," says Lopata, "and he kind of faced the pitcher and he crouched a little bit down, not as much as I did, but it came back to my mind the way he hit, so I turned around and faced the pitcher and crouched. And I think it was [in] Chicago I got two or three hits. Then we went to Milwaukee, and I got down a little lower. I got three more hits... and I kept hitting ever since."

1954 ALL-STAR GAME

THE 1954 All-Star Game was a wild affair. The lead went back and forth between the AL and the NL. Dean Stone entered the game in the top of the eighth with the AL behind 9–8, two outs, and runners on first and third. Facing Duke Snider, Stone threw a couple of pitches

and then the runner at third tried to steal home. Stone threw him out, the inning was over, and the side was retired.

The AL regained the lead in the bottom of the eighth, and Virgil Trucks, who pitched the ninth, preserved the lead. When all was said and done, a total of 20 runs had been scored—an All-Star Game record. The AL won 11–9. And who do you think was the winning pitcher? It was Stone, who had not retired a single batter.

"I didn't even know that I had won until we were sitting in the clubhouse and people started talking about me winning it," says Stone. "They took me out; I went to the clubhouse, and pretty soon they said I'd won it."

1954 INDIANS

COMING OFF three consecutive 90+ win second-place finishes under Al Lopez, the '54 Indians finished with an incredible 111-43 record. The Yankees won 103 games, which would have easily led to a pennant most other years, but in '54 it left them 8 games behind.

The Indians had a monumentally talented pitching staff. It featured four future Hall of Famers—Early Wynn, Bob Feller, Bob Lemon, and Hal Newhouser—whose combined record was 66-23. The overall team ERA was 2.78. With the slugging power of Larry Doby and Al Rosen, and the league leading .341 batting

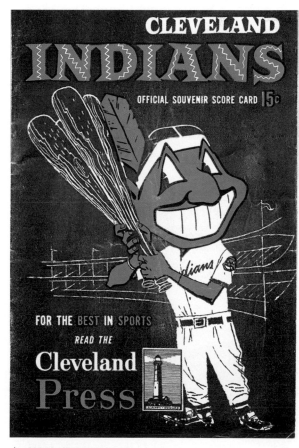

★ **1954 Indians scorecard.** Author's collection

average of Bobby Avila, the Indians crushed everyone. Fans could still taste the sweet 1948 World Series victory against the Boston Braves.

Yet for all their accomplishments, they were swept 4–0 by the Giants in the World Series. Their momentum was halted in the first game when Willie Mays made a spectacular back-to-home-plate catch of a fly ball hit by Vic Wertz to deep center field. The play came to be known in baseball lore simply as "The Catch."

"We won our pennant too early," says '54 Indian Wally Westlake. "The Giants went right down to the last day, and they come into that series with their asses on fire, and they just about kicked us out of the town. They whomped on us pretty good."

"I wouldn't say we were overconfident," says pitcher Don Mossi. "We were kind of, I guess, *stale* you might say." The series was a big disappointment for the team. Slugger Al Rosen puts it this way: "It was a natural disaster, and something I'd like to be able to erase forever. But I can't."

It would be 51 years before Cleveland made it to another World Series.

THE BIGGEST TRADE

AFTER THE 1954 season, the Yankees were pennant-hungry. On December 2, they finalized a 17-player deal with the newly created Orioles.

It was the largest trade in baseball history. The trade saw Don Larsen go to the Yanks, where he would pitch a perfect game in the World Series two years later.

Don E. Leppert was in the Yankees farm system when he was traded: "I was summoned up, and went to spring training with Baltimore and actually opened up the season against the Washington Senators in 1955, Opening Day. President Eisenhower threw the first ball out."

BYE-BYE BROWNS, A'S, AND BRAVES!

THOUGH RARELY a winning team, the St. Louis Browns nonetheless had a devoted following and a long history dating back to 1902. But after their first pennant in 1944, and despite Bill Veeck's best efforts, the Browns were unable to achieve any further magic. Veeck sold the team, and after the 1953 season, the franchise relocated to Baltimore and became the Orioles.

Ed Mickelson, who had the Browns' last RBI, remembers the end: "That last year with the Browns, they won 54, and on the last day of the season, they lost 100. I played in the last game of the season, and I drove in the last run for the Browns, and the score was 1–0 in the seventh inning, and I'm playing first base in the last game. I didn't know it was gonna be the last ever for the Browns, but there was a lot of ru-

Author's collection

mors that it would. So I'm thinking, *I drove in the winning run for the Browns, we win 1–0.* And in the top of the seventh Jungle Jim [Rivera] hits a home run up in the right field pavilion, 1–1.... We lost the game 2–1 in 11 innings."

The end was in sight for the Philadelphia Athletics, too. With Connie Mack finally retired, control of the team went to his sons, who sold the crumbling team, which only drew 304,000 fans in 1954. The team was reborn in '55 as the Kansas City A's (who moved to California in 1968).

After the 1952 season, the seventh-place Boston Braves moved to Milwaukee. "When we came to Milwaukee," says Johnny Logan, "everybody was asking me, what kind of a team does Boston have? And I said, 'I think a pretty good one.'" He was right. The Braves finished second in '53 and won the pennant in '57 and '58 before moving to Atlanta in 1966.

THE WORST BLOWOUT

On April 23, 1955, the Chicago White Sox scored 29 runs on 29 hits, including seven home runs and five doubles, against the Kansas City Athletics in Kansas City. It was the most runs ever scored by an American League team—a record that would stand until 2007 when the Texas Rangers scored 30 runs against the Baltimore Orioles. Starting pitcher Bobby

ACTIVITY

Longest Throw

IN 1910, LARRY LEJEUNE set a new record for long-distance throwing when he rifled a ball 426 feet, 6.25 inches. Lejeune's record stood for more than four decades, until Don Grate broke it in 1952 with a throw that traveled 434 feet. Grate broke his own record on August 23, 1953, by throwing 443 feet, 3.5 inches, and then again a few days later on August 27, his 33rd birthday, when he reached 445 feet and 1 inch.

In this activity you will hold your own throwing contest and see how far you can throw and how it compares to Grate's feat.

You Will Need
★ An open field
★ Measuring tape
★ A baseball
★ A couple dozen white plastic knives
★ A permanent marker
★ Several friends

Allow each participant five throws. Write the name of each participant on five of the plastic knives and give them to an observer. The observer will mark where each throw first lands by sticking a knife in the ground at that spot. Measure and record in a notebook the distances of each participant's five throws. The longest throw will be the one that counts.

Now, how much farther to 445 feet?

Shantz gave up 9 runs in just 1⅔ innings. By the time the sixth A's pitcher, Ozzie Van Brabant, came into the game in the eighth, the score was a whopping 27–6.

What do you do in that situation? Van Brabant says, "You're taking a beating, and you wipe the blood off the ball and try to put a hex on it that nobody gets another base hit off you. You do the best that you possibly can, and you hope that the bats ran out of hits."

GO AHEAD, TAKE FIRST

WALKS HAVE been given out since the early days of baseball. Nearly all of the time a walk is completely unintentional. Walking a batter is usually the last thing a pitcher wants to do. But there are times when walking someone has benefits. For example, with a runner on second and one out, a walk would create a double play situation. Or perhaps a really hot hitter is coming up to the plate with a man on; better to put him on first than to risk him hitting a double or a home run.

These "intentional" walks have also been a part of baseball since the very beginning. Despite this long history, intentional walks, or intentional bases on balls (IBB), were only officially tracked beginning in 1955. The first recorded intentional walk was given to Randy Jackson of the Cubs by Brooks Lawrence of the Cardinals on April 12, 1955. "It was in St. Louis, the first day of the season. I guess they walked me to load the bases," says Jackson.

BATS

PLAYERS' PREFERRED bat lengths and weights usually depend on their own height and weight. Six-foot-two Babe Ruth once swung a 35½-inch-long, 54-ounce bat. Five-foot-four Wee Willie Keeler's bat was only 30½ inches and 29 ounces.

Ty Cobb rubbed his bats down with tobacco juice to season them and lock out moisture. Many players rub a sticky substance called pine tar on the bat handle to give them a better grip. The most popular bat is the Louisville Slugger, manufactured by Hillerich & Bradsby in Kentucky. Most bats used to be made of ash, but more players are requesting maple bats these days, which tend to shatter more easily.

Alex Grammas tells a story about teammate Stan Musial: "He used to order Louisville slugger bats—a certain length of course and a certain weight. And when he got in a new bat, he had a scraper, and he'd scrape the handle thinner than you could imagine. He didn't order them that way, but he'd take his scraper and scrape it down. One day I picked up one of his bats, and I walked in front of his locker.... I said, 'What happens to this bat if you hit a ball

Hard-throwing rookie Bill Oster struck out Ted Williams on four pitches the first time he faced the Boston great in 1954. In his second at bat, Williams hit a pop-fly out. In the third at bat, Williams popped a fly out ... of the park.

The only player to have been hit by a pitch in his sole plate appearance and never take the field was Fred Van Dusen of the 1955 Phillies. "They called me once," says Van Dusen. "We were losing 9–0, and they used every pinch hitter on the team except me. I was the only active player that didn't get used, and they called me. I got an opportunity to bat, and I got hit by a pitch off the knee, which didn't hurt. I took first base, and the next guy made an out. That was my only at bat."

on the fist?' He looked at me and said, 'I don't hit no balls on the fist!' I busted out laughing."

THE AGE OF PAIGE

COUNTLESS NEGRO League stars never played in the majors, but one of the league's greatest players eventually did reach the majors—22 years after his debut!

Satchel Paige's professional baseball career began at age 20 in 1927. Over the next 20 years, he played for a number of Negro League teams. By Paige's own account he pitched in more than 2,600 games and threw 300 shutouts and 55 no-hitters. Including barnstorming and exhibition games, the super-durable Paige pitched a few innings nearly every day for 40 years.

Paige was signed by Bill Veeck's Indians in 1948 and made his first appearance on July 9 before a crowd of 78,000 in the fifth inning against the Browns. At the age of 42, he was the first African American major league pitcher (and the oldest rookie ever). It turned out to be an excellent year for Paige, who was 6-1 with a 2.48 ERA, and pitched a scoreless two-thirds of an inning in the World Series.

One of baseball's most beloved characters, "Satch" was easygoing, funny, and wise. Known for quirky windups, he once explained, "I use my single windup, my double windup, my triple windup, my hesitation windup, my

no windup. I also use my step-'n'-pitch-it, my submariner, my side-armer and my bat-dodger. Man's got to do what he's got to do."

Anyone who played with him remembers a unique man. Neil Berry, who was Paige's teammate on the 1953 Browns, tells this story: "We had spring training in Yuma, Arizona, and we traveled around down there. We stopped at Gila Bend one time for a sandwich and to get some gas for the bus. They had a big sign on the side that said No Blacks Allowed and we said, 'Come on, Satchel, if they won't allow you, we won't even go in.' So he says, 'No, no, no, no—you guys go on in and have a sandwich.' And there's the guy who's one of the highest-paid relief men in baseball, probably one of the greatest ballplayers that ever lived, sitting out there between the gas pumps with a Coke and a sandwich, and he says, 'I don't want to cause any trouble with anybody.' That's the kind of a guy he was."

Put Paige into a game and you'd never know what antics he'd pull. "One of the first times he pitched," recalls Jack Spring, Paige's teammate on the 1956 Miami Marlins, "he came in, I don't remember the score, but he was in in the ninth in a close game, two outs and a couple of guys on base. And the ball was hit right back to him. And he turned, and he started to walk toward the dugout as if he had caught a fly ball or something. And after he had taken a couple of steps he raised his left arm and without looking threw it to first

★ Satchel Paige as a member of the Kansas City Monarchs. Author's collection

Control-Freak Challenge

WITHOUT GOOD CONTROL, a pitcher can throw 100 miles per hour and still lose plenty of games. Being able to successfully pinpoint where you want the ball to go is key to fooling hitters and striking them out rather than walking them. Satchel Paige liked to demonstrate his superb control by throwing at a tiny target. As his teammate and fellow pitcher Tom Qualters recounts: "He'd take the foil from a stick of chewing gum, and he'd fold it up into a little square, and he would set that on the corner of the plate, and then he'd say, 'Now what corner of that do you want me to hit?' And then cause we were all on him, giving him a bunch of crap, he'd go into some crazy windup, and he'd throw [it] right over the corner of that little piece of foil. That's how good he was."

Try your hand and see how you do.

You Will Need

★ Tennis ball
★ Stick of gum
★ A group of friends
★ Measuring tape

Take a stick of gum out of its wrapper, open up the wrapper flat, and then fold it into quarters. Place the wrapper on the ground. Start off just a few feet away from the wrapper, and try to toss the ball directly over it. At a minimum, the ball has to pass over a corner of the foil wrapper. Record how many tries out of 10 you make it from 5 feet away. The lowest score drops out of the contest.

Now back up to 10 feet and try again, eliminating the person with the fewest hits again. Next try throwing from 15 feet and then 20. Increase by increments of 5 feet until there is a winner.

base for the out, and Don Osborn, who was the manager, he about fainted in the dugout."

Paige played in 1948 and 1949 with Cleveland, then from 1951 to 1953 with the Browns. From 1956 to 1958, he was in the minors with AAA Miami. Signed by Charlie Finley to the Athletics in 1965, Paige appeared in one game at the age of 59. He pitched three innings and allowed one hit and no runs. In a move orchestrated by Finley before the game, Paige sat in a rocking chair in the bullpen during the game while a "nurse" stood watch over him.

PERFECT!

DON LARSEN had little success with the Browns and Orioles his first two years pitching in the majors, ending up with a 10-33 record. His fortunes reversed when he was traded to the Yankees, and he went 9-2 in 1955 and 11-6 in 1956.

When the 1956 postseason came, it wasn't a certainty that Larsen would see action. In the 1955 World Series, he'd started a game and given up five runs in four innings. In game two of the 1956 series, Larsen lasted only 1⅔ innings. He gave up four runs in a game the Yankees would lose 11–8. Despite that, Larsen got another start in game five with the series tied at two games apiece. Sal Maglie of the Dodgers pitched well, allowing just two runs on five hits. But Larsen was better.

In fact, Larsen was perfect. He didn't allow a single runner to get to first base. There were a couple of close calls: there was a hard Jackie Robinson grounder that almost got past the third baseman in the second inning, and in the fifth, Mickey Mantle made a diving catch. "They play well behind you, they save a lot of mistakes that you made," says Larsen.

After Larsen struck out the 27th batter, pinch hitter Dale Mitchell, Larsen's teammates carried him off the field in joyous celebration of his accomplishment. He'd thrown only 97 pitches. It was the only perfect game ever thrown in World Series history, a remarkable moment for a pitcher who'd led the league in losses two years earlier. What was the secret to Larsen's success? "I just tried to do my best with any club I was with," he says. "You make a good effort and keep working at it, something good's gotta happen sometime."

After a 1–0 game six loss at the hands of Clem Labine, the Yankees went on to beat the Dodgers, 4–3, winning game seven by a score of 9–0. Larsen had a few more good seasons with the Yanks and then in December 1959 was sent to Kansas City in the trade that brought Roger Maris to the Yankees. After 1961, he was used mainly as a reliever and finished his career in 1967 with an 81-91 record. In 2012, Larsen's perfect-game uniform sold at auction for $756,000.

*I*n September 1957, Ted Williams set an AL record for most consecutive times on base—16. He also holds the record for most consecutive games reaching base safely—84! Don Minnick, a Senators pitcher who walked Williams for number 15 in his streak, had this to say: "I threw him a curve ball that missed about a half an inch on the outside corner, and it was on a 3-2 pitch, and he was halfway to first base before the ball went across the plate."

Author's collection

YOST WALKS MOST

THE MOST talented man at drawing walks was not Ruth, Mantle, or Williams but Eddie Yost. Of the top 25 on the career walks list, 24 players had either at least 260 home runs or .300 averages, or both. That leaves number 11 on the list, Eddie Yost, who played from 1944 to 1962. He hit just 139 homers with a .254 batting average, but he walked 1,614 times and led the AL in walks six times! Nicknamed "The Walking Man," his career high of 151 walks in 1956 came in a year when he hit just .231.

How did he do it? "Having a good eye is very important," says Yost. "And of course knowing the strike zone. And knowing umpires. Some umpires call the pitch outside strikes, others don't call the same pitch strikes. There's no teaching anybody how to get walks. The only way you can get them is from batting and knowing when a ball is a ball and a strike is a strike. People come to me and ask me how I developed. I used to foul a lot of balls. I'd pull them. Pull them foul, pull them foul, pull them foul. Ball two, ball three, pull one foul, pull one foul, ball four."

★ THE CY YOUNG AWARD ★★★★★★★★★★★★★★★★★★★★

THE CY YOUNG AWARD is the game's greatest pitching honor. Introduced in 1956, it's named after the pitcher with the most wins in history: 511. In selecting a Cy Young winner, ERA and win/loss record are both taken into account. From 1956 to 1966, only one award was given. After 1966, there was one per league.

*D*uring a game against slow-working pitcher Stan Williams in 1958, Sal Maglie decided to turn the tables. When Williams came up to bat, after two quick strikes, Maglie sat down on the pitching rubber, took one shoe off, shook the dirt out of it, put it back on, then did the same with the other shoe. When Maglie was ready to pitch again, Williams called time twice . . . then proceeded to hit a home run on the next pitch.

YANKEES DOMINATE

THE YANKEES lead all teams with 40 pennants and 27 World Series victories. The Dodgers were frequent World Series opponents for the Yanks. Between 1947 and 1956, the Yankees faced the Dodgers six times, and the Yankees won all but one of those matchups.

Charlie Silvera, Yankees catcher in those days, had this thought about his team: "You had a lot of leaders. DiMaggio was a leader, and Stirnweiss, Lindell, Henrich, they were winners, and they would tell us that finishing second is nothing, and winning the World Series, that's what we played for."

The Yankees' amazing success continued. Between 1957 and 1964, with stars such as

Mantle, Maris, and Berra, the Yankees made it to the World Series every year except for 1959.

THE KC EXPRESS

THE TERRIBLE Athletics and the terrific Yankees did a lot of business with each other in the late 1950s. Before moving from Philadelphia to Kansas City, the A's had been purchased by a friend of the Yankees' owner. Between 1955 and 1961, there were 15 trades between the two teams! Some folks referred to the A's as a Yankees farm team. Thirteen Yankees on the 1960 team were former A's, including Roger Maris, Bobby Shantz, Hector Lopez, Joe DeMaestri, and Art Ditmar, all of whom made valuable contributions.

"I was in spring training, getting ready for the '57 season with Kansas City," says Ditmar. "And that's when I was traded, in spring training. In fact, I was playing golf with Yogi and Lou Kretlow, Alvin Dark. Yogi walked up on the green and said, 'Art! Welcome, teammate!' I said, 'What are you talking about?' He said, 'You just got traded to the Yankees.' I said, 'Oh my God!' I missed a three-foot putt."

Bob Cerv, who'd started his career with the Yankees, played two seasons with Kansas City and returned to New York early in 1960; pitcher Ralph Terry, who began with the Yankees in 1956, went to Kansas City in 1957 and returned to the Yanks in 1959.

BONUS BABIES

FOR YEARS, wealthy teams signed young talent to big contracts and stockpiled them in their farm systems. The "bonus rule" was created in an effort to prevent talent hording. Existing in various forms from 1946 to 1956, the rule said that if a team signed a player for more than $4,000, it had to keep the player on its big-league roster for two years, or he could be drafted by another team. The rule was reinstated in 1962, but it only had a one-year big league roster requirement.

Most "bonus babies" signed right out of high school. Bob Miller was 17 when he pitched his first game for the Tigers in 1953, and at 18, Miller became the youngest pitcher ever to win a game against the Yankees.

A few had lasting careers, but many others weren't so lucky. They appeared in only a handful of games. Though they had to be on the roster, they weren't required to play. They were too inexperienced to perform well, but at the same time, they were unable to get that much-needed experience. Jim Brady, of the 1956 Tigers, recalls with disappointment, "Nobody ever taught me anything while I was there for two years taking up space. The disappointment was the pitching coach—I never learned a thing from him. I asked him one day what's the trick in major league pitching. He says, 'For you, lefty,

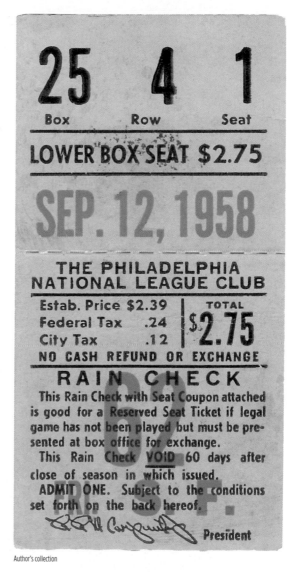

Author's collection

just rear back and fire the ball. Your ball moves and don't worry about it.' That was it."

The youngest "baby," pitcher Jim Derrington, was 16 years old when he made his major league debut for the White Sox in 1956. He appeared in his last major league game in 1957, before he even turned 18.

Tom Qualters, who signed for $40,000 with the Phillies right out of high school in 1953, had one appearance that year. After time in the minors, Qualters had a good season for the White Sox a few years later, but his major league career ended after three seasons and only 52 innings pitched.

Paul Pettit's was the most bizarre bonus baby story. Pettit was signed not by a team but by film writer/director Frederick Stephani, who gave him an $85,000 contract for the rights to his story. Stephani wanted to do a movie featuring a baseball star, but it was too expensive to get an established star. He chose Pettit thinking in a few years the pitcher would be huge, and he'd then make his movie. Stephani next got Pettit a major league contract; on January 31, 1950, Pettit signed with the Pirates for $100,000. "We were meeting in a lawyer's office in Los Angeles," said Pettit, "and we had my father, myself, my lawyer, the lawyer whose

★ **Bob Cerv was traded to the A's from New York and then back.** Author's collection

office it belonged to, and then a general manager for Pittsburgh, and the scout Tom Downey, so there were about six, seven, eight people there. And they said, 'Well, we want to sign you to a contract, and we're just going to take over the obligations of the contract for $85,000.' My dad said, 'No, we want $100,000.' So they went back into another room for 10 minutes or so, and they came back and said, 'OK, you got it.'"

The bonus frenzy reached a peak in 1964, when college star Rick Reichardt triggered a bidding war that resulted in him signing with the Angels for a whopping $205,000.

The bonus rule was discontinued in 1965, and the amateur draft was introduced. Now players were drafted by a particular club and then afterward would negotiate with them. The first draft choice in 1965, Rick Monday, signed for $100,000.

DODGERS DODGE BROOKLYN, MAKE GIANTS LEAP

DODGERS OWNER Walter O'Malley desperately wanted a new stadium for his team. In 1956, he pushed for a domed stadium in Brooklyn, but his plan was rejected. O'Malley sold Ebbets Field, and the Dodgers were just tenants in 1956 and '57. In August 1957, O'Malley announced that the Brooklyn Dodgers would no longer exist after the season ended. O'Malley

★ **THE GOLD GLOVE** ★ ★ ★ ★ ★ ★ ★ ★ ★ ★ ★ ★ ★ ★ ★ ★ ★ ★ ★

SINCE 1957, THE RAWLINGS GOLD GLOVE AWARD has been given to the best fielder at each position every season. The players with the most Gold Gloves are pitcher Greg Maddux (18), third baseman Brooks Robinson (16), and pitcher Jim Kaat (16). Good defense is half skill, half reflexes. Pitcher Bobby Shantz, who has 8 Gold Gloves, recalls: "Nellie Fox got me right in the stomach one day, but I threw him out anyway."

also convinced Giants owner Horace Stoneham to relocate to California.

"We didn't have a very good ball club in New York in '56 and '57," said Daryl Spencer of the Giants. "We had a lot of rookies and young players, and the fans were kind of getting on us, so we were all happy to leave."

The Dodgers wound up in Los Angeles in the old football coliseum before Dodger Stadium was completed, and the Giants were in San Francisco's minor league Seals Stadium before moving to Candlestick Park in 1960. Stan Williams recalls the Dodgers' new home: "It was interesting because it was a football stadium, and there was no plush seats or anything else, so all the movie stars had to sit on the bench like everybody else. We used to look over the top of the dugout and check out all the movie stars. It was quite a thrill."

The legendary New York rivalry was over. Fans mourned the loss of their teams, but both were very successful out west. The Dodgers won the pennant in '59, '63, '65, and '66, and the Giants won it in '62 and came in second from '65 to '68.

PINCHING FOR TED

PINCH HITTERS are generally used in the late innings of a close game, but using them can be a gamble. It's not easy to come off the bench cold and perform.

The best players almost never get pinch hit for. In Ted Williams's entire 19-year career, there was only one occasion when someone pinch hit for him—after he fouled a ball off his foot in 1958. Carroll Hardy, the pinch hitter, recalls, "He injured his instep. It hit him down on the instep, and it hurt him so badly he limped off the field and to the dugout and up in the clubhouse. And Pinky Higgins said, 'Hardy get a bat. You're the hitter,' and I hit into a double play to end the inning, and nobody thought a thing about it until midwinter that one of the writers said, 'Charlie, did you know that you're the only man to ever pinch hit for Ted Williams?'"

THE SLUGGING PITCHER

OVER THE years there've been a handful of pitchers who could hit exceptionally well. The game's best-slugging pitcher was Jack Harshman, who played between 1948 and 1960. After an unsuccessful stint with the Giants in 1950, Harshman clubbed 47 homers for the AA Nashville Volunteers in 1951. His road back to the majors began with advice from Nashville owner Larry Gilbert, who suggested he'd have a better chance at making it in the majors as a pitcher than as a first baseman.

Not only did Harshman succeed as a pitcher, he kept up his home run hitting. In only 424 AB, Harshman crushed 21 home runs between 1948 and 1960. Incredibly, 27.6 percent of his career hits were home runs, which for years was a record for *any* batter with over 400 AB.

Harshman says, "In 1951, I led the league in home runs, in runs batted in, runs scored, total bases, and I drove in more runs than I got hits, and I was [having] a terrifically great offensive season. And it was the same year that I was told I was going to switch to pitching. Kind of a strange set of circumstances. Matter of fact, I went back to Minneapolis in 1952 as a pitcher without any real experience at having been a pitcher."

KNUCKLEBALL SANDWICH

THE KNUCKLEBALL, a fluttering pitch whose bottom drops out as it nears the plate, has been around since the early 20th century. Because the

> The Braves of the late 1950s had the most powerful trio of home run hitters ever: Hank Aaron (755 career home runs), Eddie Mathews (512), and Joe Adcock (336). Their grand total career homers was 1,603, which surpassed the totals of the three big bats of the 1961 Yankees (Mantle, Berra, and Maris) and the 1927 Yankees (Ruth, Gehrig, and Lazzeri).

knuckler doesn't strain the arm as much as other pitches, knuckleballers, such as Hoyt Wilhelm (1952–1972), Phil Niekro (1964–1987), and Joe Niekro (1967–1988), tend to have long careers.

Though it's easy on the arm, it's not easy to throw. According to Wilbur Wood, one of the 1960s' top knuckleballers, "You've got to throw it for strikes. There are many pitchers, infielders, outfielders, that have got real good knuckleballs. But when they get on the hill and they throw it 60 feet, 6 inches, they can't throw it over for strikes, and that's the biggest problem with it."

Just the thought of the knuckleball frightens hitters. And that benefits pitchers, like Hal Brown: "I threw a lot of knuckleballs, but I didn't throw nearly as many as I got credit for. I get credit for throwing a lot more than I did because a lot of people hit a lot of bad pitches I threw because they didn't want me to get ahead of them and have to hit the knuckleball."

Catchers working with unpredictable knuckleballs also face a daunting task. One day in July 1958, each of the three Indians catchers was told that he'd be catching Hoyt Wilhelm the next day. It was only the fourth start of Wilhelm's major league career, but he already had a reputation for being impossible to catch. That night, not one of the three catchers could sleep, each feeling so agitated at the thought of catching Wilhelm.

★ **Jack Harshman.**
Author's collection

The chosen catcher, J. W. Porter, had an idea—why not use a first baseman's glove, which was much bigger than a catcher's mitt, behind the plate? This seemingly brilliant idea didn't help. In fact, in the first two innings, Porter had three passed balls. He switched back to a regular catcher's mitt and had one additional passed ball the rest of the game. The performance tied an AL record for passed balls.

REVOLUTION IN CUBA

PROFESSIONAL BASEBALL was popular in Cuba long before minor league baseball began there in 1946 with the Havana Cubans, a Class C/B team in the Florida International League that played against Florida teams. In 1954, a new AAA team, the Havana Sugar Kings, joined the International League, which also had teams from Montreal, Ottawa, and Toronto. Dozens of American ballplayers played for Havana over the years, and hundreds more visited Cuba to play against them.

During the off-season in the 1950s and '60s, many American players kept in practice and made extra money by playing "winter ball" in Colombia, Panama, Venezuela, the Dominican Republic, Cuba, and Puerto Rico.

When Fidel Castro took over Cuba in 1959, there were armed soldiers all over Havana. Ron Negray, a member of the 1959 Montreal Royals, remembers playing in Cuba that year: "The kids that were in the army, they'd take their guns to the ballpark, and anytime Havana did a good thing, they'd shoot their guns up in the air. Real bullets. All our players wore batting helmets when they went on the field."

Pandemonium broke out when shots were fired during an emotionally charged game against the Rochester Red Wings in July, and a player and a coach were grazed by bullets. Red Wing Cal Browning was a witness: "Frank Verdi got shot in the ear. They shot a bullet into the air, and it came down and hit him on the ear. I remember him being down in the third base coaching box when I went by into the clubhouse. So everybody got in, they blocked the clubhouse out, and they flew us out of there that night."

Later that year, the Sugar Kings and the Minneapolis Millers met for the Junior World Series. Castro, a baseball fan, attended. Johnny Goryl was a member of the '59 Millers: "The first game, he came in through the center field fence. If you can visualize 37,000 pulling out a handkerchief and waving it in the air yelling, 'Viva Fidel!' and the handkerchief sounded like a swarm of bees in the air in the stadium. I mean, that's how strong they were waving those handkerchiefs. It was quite an experience."

Strained relations between the United States and Cuba caused the Sugar Kings to relocate to Jersey City in 1960.

ALMOST PERFECT

IMAGINE PITCHING spectacularly and still losing! It happened in 1959 to Harvey Haddix. Haddix, who was 33 years old and in his first year with the Pirates, was having a good year: he was 4-2 with a 2.67 ERA, and four complete games.

Though Haddix had been a 20-game winner in 1953, he was up against a daunting opponent in Milwaukee's Lew Burdette. The 32-year-old Brave had also been a 20-game winner. He had led the league in ERA in 1956 and was on his way to another 20-game season in 1959. The two faced off on a windy, muggy night. Haddix had awoken that morning feeling sick with a cold and a sore throat.

Despite his ailments, by the end of the ninth, Haddix had only thrown 78 pitches and allowed no runners. It was a perfect game, but it wasn't over. The Pirates had nothing to show for their eight hits. The game continued into extra innings, as did Haddix's success. He retired the side in the 10th, 11th, and 12th innings. According to Braves infielder Johnny O'Brien, "[Haddix] always had a pretty kind of sneaky fastball, a slider, and a bit of a changeup. That night he had a spectacularly good slider. I mean, it looked like a fastball coming in, and it would dart in at the end. He was good. We only hit a couple of balls hard. I hit one, and I think Logan hit one. But everything else was kind of like a routine out."

The Pirates still didn't score. In the bottom of the 13th, the first Braves batter, Felix Mantilla, hit a ground ball and reached first on a throwing error. The play ended the perfect game for Haddix. Eddie Mathews bunted Mantilla to second, and Haddix intentionally walked Hank Aaron. Joe Adcock came to the plate next. Johnny O'Brien remembers what happened next: "The first pitch to Adcock was a slider, low and in. He took it. The second pitch was a fastball, high and away, not in the strike zone. But he was a big strong guy, and he reached out, and he hit it. It went toward right center field."

Adcock hit a home run! It was ruled a double though, because after Mantilla scored, Aaron had begun to walk off the field and Adcock passed him on the bases and was called out. But the Braves still won. The final score was 1–0. Harvey Haddix had pitched 12 perfect innings and wound up losing a 13-inning one-hitter.

COMPLETE/INCOMPLETE GAMES

THE RELIEF pitchers of old didn't see nearly as much action as today's relievers. A starter pitched the entire game unless he became injured or was being shelled by the other team.

On April 21, 1959, outfielder Don Demeter became the first player to hit three homers in a game *for* the L.A. Dodgers. On September 12, 1961, Demeter became the first player to hit three homers *against* the Dodgers.

As pitcher Paul Foytack (63 career complete games) explains, "I was talking to a man one day that recently signed with Detroit, Hal Newhouser. We were having lunch, and I said 'Hal, two years in a row, 29 complete games!' You know what he said? 'Yeah, but I started 34.'"

"We played different back when I played. Because we were so concerned about completing the game, going nine innings was the big thing with us," says Chuck Estrada, who won 18 games in 1960. "So I kind of pitched according to the score. If my teammates got me runs, then I would kind of coast. I wasn't concerned about earned run average. I was concerned about *W*s. So I would try to conserve energy to go nine innings. If the game was close, I would pitch harder."

The frequency of relievers entering a game went from almost never to almost always, especially after teams began imposing a 100-pitch limit on their starters. The 1905 Cubs threw 133 complete games, the 1920 Cubs 95, the 1960 Cubs 36, and the 2010 Cubs just 1. Most relievers through the 1960s pitched two or more innings. In the early 1970s, Orioles manager Earl Weaver was one of the first to create more specialized roles for relief pitchers.

Pete Richert, who played for Weaver, says: "We were flying on a plane going to Boston for a weekend series, and he comes to me, and he says, 'Pete look, if it's a two-run game, winning or losing, and Yastrzemski's hitting in the eighth or ninth inning, I don't even wanna call you. You're ready. You got Yastrzemski. No matter what.' And that never changed. I had Carl. And that was it. I'd come in and get Carl in the ninth inning for one out, and Watt would come in and get the two right-handed hitters, and we'd go on our way, and it was great."

Games these days often include at least one of each: a long man (sixth and seventh innings), a set-up man (eighth), and the closer (ninth). "I'd have a hard time playing today," says 1960 Cy Young–winner Vern Law (119 complete games), "because I'm not gonna let somebody else decide if I'm gonna win or not. I wanna be out there on the mound doing my job."

TRADES

BEFORE AGENTS, multiyear contracts, and trade-restriction clauses, players were the property of their clubs and could be traded anytime. To their fans' dismay, non-contending teams might ship off popular players to a pennant-chaser in exchange for prospects and cash. One star player might even be traded for another.

One of the most famous trades was made in April 1960, when the reigning AL home run champ, popular Rocky Colavito of the Indians, was sent to Detroit for the reigning AL batting champ, Harvey Kuenn. The trade made big headlines, but after a year, the Indians traded Kuenn to the Giants. Colavito wound up back in Cleveland in 1965. "It was a tough adjustment," admits Colavito. "I never let on at the time, but it was a very, very difficult time in my life, and of my career. The people in Detroit—some embraced me and some didn't. Some were Harvey Kuenn fans, and some were my fans or fans of the new player. So I wouldn't say they totally embraced me, but some did."

Some players were never traded; others were constantly packing their bags. In the course of his 20-year major league career, pitcher Bobo Newsom was traded or sold 15 times. The last occasion came in 1952 when he was 44 years old! In the space of seven months, between October 1966 and May 1967, outfielder Len Gabrielson wore the uniforms of all three California teams—the Giants, Angels, and Dodgers.

Sometimes what looks like a fair deal turns out to be a steal. In midseason 1964, pitcher Ernie Broglio of the Cardinals, who'd led the league in wins in 1960, was traded to the Cubs for a youngster named Lou Brock. The Cubs sure thought they were getting the better end of the deal. So far in his career, Brock was hitting .257 with a total of 50 stolen bases. As it turned out, Broglio's record for the rest of '64 and the two years that followed was 7-19. Brock went on to steal 938 bases. He led the league eight times and played the rest of his career with the Cards.

A trade could come any time, even between games of a doubleheader; in 1922 Chicago's Max Flack and St. Louis's Cliff Heathcote were traded between games, and both men played in both games. In 1958, Athletics shortstop Billy Hunter was traded to the Indians for Chico Carrasquel in between games of a doubleheader at Yankee Stadium. Hunter headed immediately to Baltimore but was not officially an Indian until the next day because Carrasquel was still there and in the lineup.

Bob Kuzava got traded while at a railroad station in 1950. "I was with the White Sox, and we were in St. Louis playing the St. Louis Browns— we had a doubleheader. We were at the train station, and the traveling secretary says, 'Hey, you just got traded to the Washington Senators!' So I said, 'OK.' I went back to Chicago, got my wife, and I had two kids then, and brought them back here to Wyandotte, then I went over to Washington. Sometimes you'd hear it on the radio instead of from somebody from the ball club. That's the way it was."

When pitcher Dick Hall was traded from the Pirates to the Athletics in December 1959, he went from the team that would win the 1960 World Series to one that would finish last. Catcher Hal Smith, who was on the flip side of the trade, left Kansas City behind and hit .295 for the pennant-winning Pirates. In 1968, shortstop Ron Hansen was traded from the

*P*irate reliever Elroy Face was 18-1 in 1959. This .947 winning percentage is the best for *any* pitcher ever, and Face didn't start any games. For Face to win, the Pirates had to take the lead in the late innings . . . 18 times. Of course, there was that one pesky loss, which came on September 11 against Chuck Churn of the Dodgers. Churn was Face's former teammate. Face says: "The batter broke his bat on the winning hit, and it dribbled between third and short for a base hit."

Senators to the White Sox three days after turning an unassisted triple play and the day after hitting a grand slam.

Players were often the last to hear they'd been traded. In June 1948, Dodger Don Lund was at home in Brooklyn reading the newspaper, while his wife was fixing dinner, when he called out to her, "Hey dear, I noticed we just got traded!" In a couple of days, he was suited up as a St. Louis Brown. Bud Thomas was in Puerto Rico in the winter of 1951, standing in front of his hotel, when a man came up to him and told him that the *Sporting News* said he'd been sold from the Browns to Toronto.

Yankee Bill Renna was playing winter ball in Puerto Rico after the 1953 season when a sports writer told him he'd been traded to the Athletics. Terry Fox, who went from the Tigers to the Phillies in 1966, said, "We left Detroit and went to Cleveland, and that night we were taking batting practice. I come out there on the field, and I could see nobody wants to come stand around and talk by me. They all knew ahead of time that something was happening, but I hadn't received any word."

J. W. Porter, a catcher for the Tigers, was driving from his home in California to spring

★ **Billy Hunter packs after being traded between games of a doubleheader in 1958.** Author's collection

training in Lakeland, Florida, when he passed through Tucson, Arizona. Noting that the Indians trained there, Porter thought, *Wouldn't it be nice to play for them?* When he was finally almost in Lakeland, he stopped at a restaurant for breakfast and saw a man reading the sports pages, and something caught his attention: "Jim Hegan traded to Detroit for J. W. Porter." He'd been traded to the Indians and had to make his was back to Tucson!

Some trades were so surprising that the players didn't believe it. Randy Jackson, who went from the Cubs to the Dodgers after the 1955 season, says, "In December, I got a call from a sportswriter friend of mine, and I'd already played five years with the Cubs. And he said, 'You've been traded!' I said, 'What?' He said, 'Yeah, you've been traded!' I said, 'Well, to who?' He said, 'Well, guess!' I said, 'Oh, well, Pittsburgh?' 'No' 'St. Louis?' 'No.' I said, 'Well, get over and tell me!' He said, 'You've been traded to the Dodgers!' I said, 'You are teasing me!' You know, you play baseball, and you like the teams you're playing on, but the ideal thing is to play on a winner. Play in a World Series. And the Dodgers were always in the World Series.

And I told him, I said, 'You're teasing.' He said, 'No, you've been traded for three guys.' And I said 'Fantastic!'"

Ed Bressoud went from the Mets to the Cardinals in 1967: "I was called into the office by Wes Westrum, the manager, and he said, 'We traded you.' It was an April Fool's, first day of April. He said, 'We traded you to St. Louis,' and I'm thinking to myself, *Wait, I'm going from ninth place to first place, that's a pretty good April Fool's joke on me.*"

Chuck Kress was traded from thc Tigers to the Dodgers in 1954: "When I was told to join the Dodgers out in St. Louis, they were playing the Cardinals. So I reported to St. Louis and Walter [Alston] called me into the office and said, 'Charlie, I got a little problem.' He said, 'I may want to use you today, but I'd have to sign you to a contract.' And he said, 'I don't know what they're gonna pay you.' And we just sat there and looked at each other for a while, and he said, 'As a favor to me, would you sign a blank contract?' I said, 'You could put a dollar on there, Walter, and then I'm stuck.' 'Well,' he said, 'you'll just have to trust me, Charlie.' I said, 'All right,' and I did. I signed a blank contract."

*W*ind was the reason three players were traded from the Giants in 1959! In anticipation of the new Candlestick Park, favorable to left-handed batters due to the wind, two right-handed batters and a right-handed pitcher were traded to the Orioles in exchange for two left-handed pitchers.

EXPANSION

The 1960s was a time of change for the United States and for baseball. Babe Ruth's single-season home run record fell to an unlikely hero, segregation finally ended, and the leagues expanded twice, first in 1961 and again in 1969. Much of the decade was a pitcher's era with 1968 featuring some of the most amazing performances in baseball history.

WILLIAMS RETIRES

By the late 1950s, Ted Williams had almost reached 500 home runs, despite having missed practically five seasons due to military service. Williams won a batting title in 1957, hitting .388 and clobbering 38 homers at the age of 38. His .328 in 1958 was 60 points lower but still good enough for his sixth batting title.

Williams began 1959 recovering from a pinched nerve. By May 26, he was batting just .163 with no home runs. In mid-June, manager Pinky Higgins benched Williams for a few days on account of his weak hitting. It was the first time Williams had ever been benched. Williams said, "I got off to a bad start last year and won the batting championship, so why should I call it quits?" In July, he reinjured his neck. Williams ended 1959 at .254, his lowest average ever.

Williams regained his old form in 1960, batting over .300 after June 10, and hitting number 500 on June 17. By September 28, he had 28 homers. He sat out the next series, against the Yankees in New York, and finished his career in Boston. When Williams came to the plate for the last time in the eighth inning on that day at Fenway Park, he was 0 for 2 with a walk. Teammate Ted Wills remembers the home run that followed: "He hit one that was held up by the wind, and he said to the whole dugout, he

said, 'Next time I'm gonna knock the hell out of it. I'm gonna knock it clear out of here.' And by God, he did."

Teammate Carroll Hardy replaced Williams the next inning: "Pinky Higgins motioned to me to come over. He wanted to talk to me, and I went over, and he said, 'I want you to wait, and Ted will go out to left field. And once he goes out there, you go ahead and replace him.' [Ted] thought I was gonna go in before he went out there. He went out there; they wanted to see him appreciate the fans and all that. He got out there, and I went out, and they booed me all the way out, and cheered him all the way in, but he still never would tip his hat to them. He never acknowledged the fans." To the very end, Williams stuck to a vow he'd made back in his early days when Boston fans had booed him.

MAZ WINS IT

One of baseball's most exciting moments came during the 1960 World Series. With the series tied at three games apiece, both the Yankees and Pirates were hungry for the title. The Yankees hadn't won the pennant in 1959, and the Pirates had worked hard to rise from one of the worst records in history to a pennant eight years later. "We had a lot of desire and a lot of camaraderie on that team," says Pirates left fielder Bob Skinner.

> *I*n a bizarre move, manager Jimmy Dykes of the Tigers was traded midseason 1960 for manager Joe Gordon of the Indians.

It was an exciting game seven on October 13, 1960. The Pirates took the lead in the eighth inning by scoring five runs. The Yankees, however, rallied for two runs in the top of the ninth to tie the score. The game was tied 9–9 in the bottom of the ninth as Bill Mazeroski, the Pirates' second baseman, came up to lead off the inning. On a 1-0 pitch from reliever Ralph Terry, Mazeroski, not known as a power hitter, hit a long fly ball to left field. Teammate Bob Friend recalls the moment: "I was in the dugout. Didn't look like it was gonna make it; Berra was drifting back to the wall, but the ball was way over his head. He gave us a little scare there. I thought he was gonna catch it."

"He had good power, Maz," says Skinner. "He didn't hit a lot of home runs, but when he hit one, it went. I can still see it going back to the 405 mark and the ball clearing the wall." Pirates catcher Bob Oldis remembers the scene on the field after the homer: "I don't think he knew he hit it until he got to second base, and then I think he slowed up, and by then, we was all there. And it couldn't have happened to a nicer guy."

Just like that, the Pirates had won the World Series and Mazeroski had assured himself a place in baseball history.

As for the Yankees, well, there was shock all around. Pitcher Ralph Terry spoke to Casey Stengel after the game. "I felt bad for Stengel," recalls Terry. "I said, 'Casey, I'm sorry it ended that way for you,' because we all sort of knew he was saying goodbye, that he was fired, even before the last game. And he said before the game, he had a little meeting, 'Boys, you had a great year. I won't get to say goodbye to all of you, 'cause everybody will be going different directions when this game's over. I'll have to go on TV with Murtagh to either congratulate him or him congratulate me. I just wanted you to know, you had a great year and so forth. Have a good off-season.' And I went in and talked to him after the game. I felt bad for Casey. He said, 'Well, how were you trying to pitch him?' I said, 'I was trying to pitch him low and outside. I couldn't get the ball down.... Everything was high.' And he said, 'Well as long as you pitch, you're not always gonna get the ball where you want to. That's a physical mistake.' And he said,

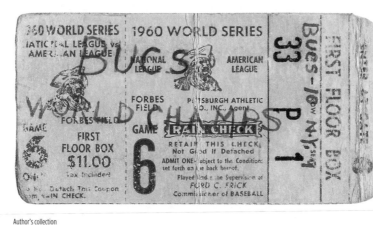

Author's collection

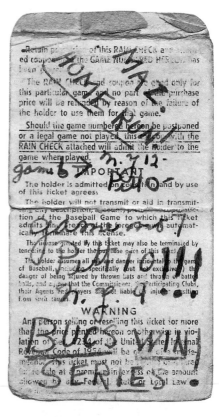

Home Run Derby

IN 1960, A TELEVISION SHOW called *Home Run Derby* pitted the hottest sluggers of the day against each other. Filmed at cozy Wrigley Field in Los Angeles (home of the minor league L.A. Angels), there were nine "innings" per contest, consisting of three "outs" per inning. Anything but a home run was an out—whether a ground ball, long fly ball, or a strike. A home run counted as one run. Whoever had the highest score at the end of the game was the winner. The winner took home $2,000 and was invited back the next week to face a new challenger. A play-by-play announcer called the shots as players such as Rocky Colavito, Bob Cerv, Harmon Killibrew, Willie Mays, Ernie Banks, and Hank Aaron batted.

Bob Cerv remembers his time on the show: "First time, I think I beat Frank Robinson, and then Bob Allison beat me 3–2 in extra innings. The next day I was so sore. You know, I didn't do much since the season ended [in] October, and then I got a call, come back and hit in the *Home Run Derby*, so I went back to California. I think I was living in Colorado then, and I went. The first day I was in it, the next day I was so sore I said I don't know if I can play today. I crawled into a tub of hot water and sat there for a couple of hours. I wasn't very strong the next day.... I had blisters on my hands. If I'd have known about it before then I'd have practiced a little."

This show was the inspiration for the home run contests that are now part of the All-Star Game. In this activity you will re-create *Home Run Derby*.

You Will Need
★ Bat(s), baseballs or softballs, and gloves
★ 7 or more participants
★ Video capabilities
★ Ball field or open area to play

Designate one participant as the home plate umpire, one as the announcer, two as the sluggers, one as catcher, one as pitcher, one as recorder, and another (optional) as outfield umpire. Pick a spot that will signify a home run. Have the recorder stand off to the third base side and film the action. The umpire should call "out!" when the batter is out, and the announcer should keep the score and provide commentary to the viewers.

'Forget it, kid. Come back and have a good year next year.'"

SANDY KOUFAX

ONE OF the biggest catcher/pitcher success stories is that of Norm Sherry and Sandy Koufax of the L.A. Dodgers. After Sherry told a young and wild Koufax to take something off his fastball in 1961, Koufax began to have much better control and strike out many more batters.

"He's reaching back and throwing," explains Sherry, "and each fastball he threw was higher and higher and out of the strike zone. Nobody was swinging. So I went out to the mound. Now we had the bases loaded, and I said to him, 'Sandy, these guys aren't swinging the bats.' I said, 'Why don't you take something off the ball, and let them hit it. We've got guys out there who'll catch the balls, and we'll get some outs. Otherwise they're not gonna swing. Let's just take something off and lay it in there and let

> **JOE AZCUE, CATCHER:** *"You've got a split second for the pitcher to throw the ball to you, a split second to see the ball, to swing the bat, a split second to throw them out. Everything is done in about 3.5 seconds."*

'em hit it.' Now I go back behind the plate… and he strikes out the side."

Koufax, who had a 36-40 record up to that point, had a 129-47 record during the rest of his career. He strung together six of the best consecutive years any pitcher has ever had. In addition, he led the league in ERA five times, in strikeouts four times, and in wins three times and won three Cy Young Awards before an ailing back forced him to retire at the age of 30.

THE COLLEGE OF COACHES

After a dismal 1960 season, Cubs owner Philip Wrigley decided to try a new approach. Instead of a single manager, Wrigley employed a group of coaches, each of whom would get a chance to be "head coach." This "College of Coaches" would run the major and minor league ball clubs in rotating fashion.

Jerry Kindall was on the 1961 Cubs: "The season began with Vedie Himsl as the head coach. And he appointed three of the eight to stay with him on the coaching staff, and the other three or four, they went to the minor leagues, each of them to a different minor league team for the Cubs. And we had a play book that Elvin Tappe had put together, one of the eight, a good baseball man, that was distributed throughout the minor leagues to all the players and coaches. And the idea, the dream, was to have everybody

doing the same thing on cutoffs, relays, double-steal defenses, bunt defenses. Every phase of the game offensively and defensively was to be done exactly the same way, all the way up through the Cubs."

The strange strategy didn't succeed. The Cubs finished seventh in the NL in 1961 and ninth in the expansion year of 1962. The system officially ended in 1965 with the appointment of veteran manager Leo Durocher as the new Cubs skipper.

★ **The College of Coaches, 1961.** Author's collection

FOUR IN A ROW

BASEBALL IS a game of firsts, but some firsts came surprisingly late in the history of the game. For example, the first time that four batters came to the plate and hit consecutive home runs was in June 1961. According to Frank Thomas of the 1961 Braves, "I was the first ballplayer ever in major league history to have been the fourth player to hit a home run in succession. When I was with Milwaukee, Mathews hit the first one off Maloney, Aaron hit the second one off Maloney, they brought in Marshall Bridges to pitch to Adcock, he hit the third one, and I hit the fourth one. First time it was ever done in baseball."

It happened six more times between 1963 and 2008.

EXPANSION

FOR DECADES there'd been eight teams per league, but everything changed in 1961 when the Los Angeles Angels and Washington Senators (the original Senators had become the Minnesota Twins) were created. The change increased the AL to 10 teams.

To populate these new teams, an expansion draft was held in December 1960. Each existing AL team could "protect" 25 players on their roster. The unprotected ones (often veteran play-

ers) could be drafted by the expansion teams. The new teams paid $75,000 per player. Picks alternated back and forth until both teams had enough players.

The Angels' first pick was Yankees pitcher Eli Grba, and the Senators' first pick was another Yankees pitcher, former MVP Bobby Shantz. Depleted clubs turned to their farm system to fill the holes the draft had created. For lucky Rollie Sheldon, who went 15-1 for the Auburn Yankees in 1960, it meant a call-up straight from D ball after only one season.

"It was a bittersweet type of thing," says Grba. "The Yankees had Maris and Cerv and everybody was coming back from 1960. And now Stengel was gone, and one of my idols, really, a man I liked, Ralph Houk, was gonna manage, and I thought, *Well, goodness!* But I was number one, and it was a new type of team. It was a bunch of guys thrown together from other organizations. It was a lot of fun."

Meanwhile, the NL added two teams in 1962. New York got the Metropolitans, and Houston got a franchise called the Colt .45s (later the Astros). This time there were three pricing levels for players: $50,000, $75,000, and $125,000.

Houston's first pick was Giants infielder Ed Bressoud and the Mets' first pick was another Giant, Hobie Landrith. Bressoud wound up on the Red Sox after Houston's manager and Boston's manager arranged a trade—shortstop

Bressoud would go to Boston, and Houston would get Boston's shortstop, Don Buddin.

Bob Aspromonte, an original Colt .45, recalls: "The Dodgers put me up for the draft. They didn't think no one would take me right away 'cause I was a young kid, and they had some established names. But Paul Richards grabbed me right away in the draft for the Houston Colt .45s. It was a great opportunity for me—a new franchise, new town, never had Major League Baseball before. And I fit in so well. It was a great experience to be the first hit, the first RBI, the first home run. All the firsts. I did all the firsts."

In their first season, the Angels placed eighth at 70-91, and the Senators were tied for ninth at 61-100. In 1962, Houston finished eighth at 64-96, which was ahead of the 59-103 Cubs. The Angels shocked everyone by being in the pennant race and finishing third in 1962, their second year of existence.

MEET THE METS

New York City's baseball fans were so excited when the year 1962 brought a new National League team. They were led by lovable but incomprehensible Casey Stengel, who'd left the Yankees two years earlier. Original Met John DeMerit recalls that first spring training: "Every morning at spring training, [Stengel] was out

*D*ue to a mix-up over draft rules in 1960, AL president Joe Cronin ordered four immediate trades to correct the mistakes. The Angels drafted Coot Veal from the Indians but were forced to quietly trade him to Washington for one of its draft picks, Ken Aspromonte. Just how secretive were these trades? Aspromonte first learned he'd been traded 53 years afterward.

★ **Colt .45 players at spring training, 1962.** Author's collection

there on the dot talking to sportswriters, and the rest of what was going on was totally ignored by the sports people. They wanted their candid quote for the day, and he was great at that. A lot of mumbo jumbo and they didn't know what he was talking about half the time; they'd have to ask each other what he meant. It was kinda like a circus."

Original Met Felix Mantilla says, "When I went to spring training with them we looked pretty decent. During spring training, I thought we would do better than what we did during the regular season. But it was a great experience. I enjoyed the year I played there."

After March, the circus headed to New York. The Mets played at the old Polo Grounds, site of the glory days of the old Giants, but there was no glory for these Mets. No, the '62 Mets were lovable losers. They finished in last place. Their record was 40-120, and they were 60½ games out of first place. The ninth-place team was 18 games ahead of them in the standings. The pitchers had a 5.04 team ERA, and the hitters had a combined .240. When the season ended, Casey Stengel said, "Imagine, 40 games I won with this club—40. That's what I used to lose with the Yankees!"

Solly Hemus was one of the '62 Mets' original coaches: "Casey was not very happy, and I wasn't very happy either, and neither were the ballplayers. They were adamant about trying to win.... They played their hearts out. They didn't give up. They just run out of gas, really. They gave their all. I'm sure they looked bad, some of the plays they made. But they weren't kidding around when they went out there. They went out to win."

BASE STEALING

Ty Cobb stole 96 bases in 1915. For a long time Cobb's record was untouchable. In 1938, Stan Hack's 16 stolen bases was good enough for the NL lead! Even among the fastest players, stolen bases simply weren't that common. One reason may have been that the balk rule, which prevents pitchers from tricking runners, was not enforced as strictly then.

"When I was playing, the pitcher could do most anything to deceive the runner like he was going to the plate and then throw to first base,"

*B*efore expansion, teams faced each opponent 22 times over 154 games. With more teams, the schedule had to be expanded. At 162 games, each team would face its opponents 18 times. The AL adopted this change in 1961 and the NL in 1962.

★ **Lady Met pin, 1960s.** Author's collection

says Gil Coan, an outfielder in the 1940s and '50s. "At that time they could step directly toward home and throw to first."

Things changed beginning in the 1960s when Maury Wills stole 104 for the 1962 Dodgers. Lou Brock (1974), Rickey Henderson (1980), and Vince Coleman (1985) followed in breaking the 100 mark.

61 IN '61

MINNESOTA-BORN ROGER Maris debuted with the Indians in 1957, playing part of 1958 with them before getting traded to the mediocre Athletics. In his first year, he batted an unimpressive .235 and hit 14 homers. His average improved slightly the next year, and his home run production doubled to 28. In 1959, Maris was still in Kansas City, where he improved his batting average to .274 but only hit 16 home runs.

After 1959, Maris was traded to the Yankees. Learning to pull the ball, he took advantage of the close right field fence. His slugging average in 1960 was a league leading .581, with 39 home runs and 112 RBIs. He even beat out teammate Mickey Mantle (40 homers/94 RBIs) for the MVP Award.

"The funny thing was that at Indianapolis, in Cleveland, and in Kansas City, we didn't really consider him a home run hitter," says

Bud Daley, Maris's teammate on four different teams. "We considered him more of a great defensive outfielder, which he was, and he could run really good. And he was just a good hitter at that time. And then when he went to New York, they told him they wanted him to pull everything, and he learned how to pull everything, and he hit."

When 1961 dawned, fans anticipated another great year—from their team and especially from Maris and Mantle. Maris got off to a slow start, but things turned around in mid May when Maris hit home runs in four consecutive games. By the end of June, Maris had 27 homers to Mantle's 25. By the end of July, Maris had 40 homers, which was more than his entire total for 1960. Would he be able to continue his slugging onslaught in the second half? He hit only one homer in early August but then clobbered seven homers in six consecutive games between August 11 and 16. Numbers 47 and 48 came against Billy Pierce of the White Sox in game 119.

Heading into September, Maris had 51 homers to Mantle's 48. Mantle, however, who missed a few games due to a hip injury, only hit two home runs between September 9 and the end of the season, which left Maris to chase the record on his own. Some were upset about the home run barrage and wanted Babe Ruth's record to stand forever—if it *had* to fall, they

ACTIVITY
Foul Ball!

IT WOULD SEEM TO MAKE SENSE that when you hit a ball, it's going to travel forward. But there are several complicating factors. For one, both the ball and the bat are round.

If a ball in the center of the strike zone is met perfectly on the bat's sweet spot, five to seven inches from the end of the barrel, it should travel straight toward center field. If a batter meets the ball too early, it will go sailing into the left or right field stands. A ball that does not make full contact with the bat might be popped up high above the infield, bounced on the ground, or fly backward. Foul balls are common because it's difficult to make solid, timely contact with 95 mph fastballs or with 78 mph off-speed pitches when you're expecting a fastball.

The next time you watch a game, record how many pitches are thrown and of those how many are foul balls. You'll be surprised to discover what percentage of all pitches are fouled off during an average game. To be even more precise, record whether the batter is right or left handed and which direction each foul ball goes. Patterns should emerge.

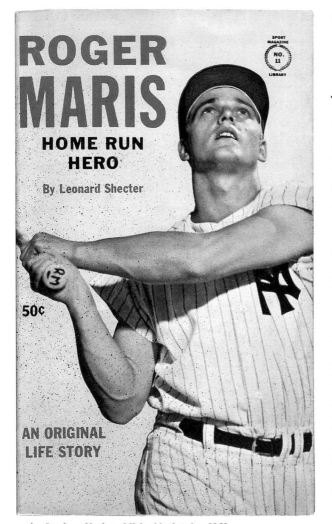

wanted Mantle to be the one to do it. The spotlight was harsh. The stress made Maris's hair begin to fall out. It didn't help that on July 17, Commissioner Ford Frick, who'd been a close friend of Babe Ruth's, announced that in his opinion, if Maris did not beat the record in the same 154 games that Ruth had hit 60, there should be a mark next to Maris's name in the record books.

The pressure was almost too much to bear. The reporters were incessant. According to teammate Bob Cerv, "What bothered Maris more than anything was how they bugged him.... He'd be out on the field working out and they'd say, 'Come on in. We want to talk to you!'"

Game 154 came, and Maris hit one home run, giving him 59. Milt Pappas was the pitcher: "I happened to see Roger and Mickey the night before the game, walking out of the clubhouse, and I walked up to Roger, and I told him what my plan was. I told him, 'I'm gonna throw you nothing but fastballs. And if I'm shaking my head, I'm calling off the slider or the changeup.' And he said, 'Are you serious?' I said, 'Yes I am, I want to see you break the record.' Mickey looked at me and said, 'What about me?' I said, 'Go to hell, Mickey. You don't need any help!' Roger did hit one that night, hit 59, and then [Richards] took me out of the game. He just missed the first time up. He hit one right up almost against the wall, and the second one he hit out."

Reliever Dick Hall faced Maris after Pappas left the game: "We'd been debating ahead of time. If you get in that situation, are you gonna pitch to him and have your name go down in history? I gave up the 61st home run to Roger Maris? Half the guys said, 'Man, no, I'll walk him every time; I don't want to have that kind of notoriety.' But myself and some of the others said, 'No, I'm gonna give him my best stuff, and what happens, happens.' And actually, I pitched to him twice. I struck him out once, and he hit a line drive, hit it hard, but right at the right fielder the second time up. And I threw a lot of pitches to him, and every single pitch was a strike or close enough that he swung at it."

On September 21, in an article titled "Babe's 60 Stands Again," the Associated Press reported: "Roger Maris' relentless assail on Babe Ruth's hallowed home run record ended in defeat Wednesday night." Maris smacked number 60 on September 26 and hit number 61 in the final game of the season, on October 1. The 19-year-old truck driver who caught the ball won $5,000, and Maris won the MVP Award for a second straight year.

So how would Babe Ruth have felt about his record falling? According to his daughter Julia, "Daddy said, when any of his records were broken, 'Records were made to be broken.' Everybody is always trying to set a new record, and he said that's what the game is all about."

Maris would never be the same again. The strain of the '61 season had taken its toll. In 1962 he hit just 33 home runs. As time passed, Maris's record became more accepted as legitimate. Still, by the time Maris died in 1985, he hadn't received the full recognition he deserved.

So what's the bottom line on Maris? His teammate Johnny Gray sums it up: "I thought he was one of the most solid ballplayers I ever met in my life. I thought if I was ever manager of a ball club, I'd like to have every player like Roger Maris, because he came to the ballpark like a man coming to work that wanted to become president of a bank. He worked his fanny off all the time. He came to the ballpark to play ball, and that was it."

FISCHER'S NO-WALK ZONE

BACK IN 1913, Giants pitcher Christy Mathewson set a record by going 68 innings without walking anyone. The record stood for almost 50 years until A's pitcher Bill Fischer topped it in the summer of 1962. Beginning August 3, Fischer went 84.1 innings, spread over 14 games, without walking anyone. That's 350 batters in a row! Fischer walked only 8 in 127 innings the entire season yet all he had to show

Author's collection

for it was a 4-12 record. Ironically, during his streak, one of his opponents almost pitched a perfect game against the Athletics; a walk in the ninth inning spoiled it.

When did people begin to take notice of his amazing streak? According to Fischer, "I pitched a game in Chicago, and I got taken out. And then, when I was sitting in the dugout, they put up on the scoreboard, it said: 'Fischer has now gone 50 innings without a walk,' and everybody else took off on it."

> **L**eft-handed hitters generally do better against right-handed pitchers, and vice versa. Switch hitters, as they are known, are therefore quite valuable. The greatest switch hitter was Mickey Mantle, whose numbers batting righty were .330 with 161 home runs and .280 with 369 home runs from the left. Other great switch hitters include Pete Rose, Tim Raines, Eddie Murray, Frankie Frisch, and Chipper Jones.

★ LEFT: The president traditionally attended Opening Day in Washington and threw a ball from the stands, which players would then scramble for. Courtesy of the National Archives (6817167)

★ BELOW: Here President Kennedy is seen signing a ball for a lucky Marty Kutyna in 1962. Courtesy of Marty Kutyna

THE SECOND DEAD BALL ERA

Beginning in 1963, batting averages took a big dip that lasted about 10 years. The low point was in 1968 when the AL average was only .230! That year, AL teams hit almost 450 fewer home runs than in 1962. There is no single explanation for the prolonged dip in averages. Possible factors include mediocre expansion teams, an expanded strike zone, and excellent pitching from the likes of Sandy Koufax, Denny McLain, Bob Gibson, Sam McDowell, and Tom Seaver.

It was good for pitchers... to a point. "When you can't win 20 games with a 1.81 ERA, and I had 283 strikeouts in 270 innings, you aren't getting any runs," says Sam McDowell of his 1968 season. Between 1947 and 1962, the *only* pitcher in the majors to achieve an ERA under 2.00 was Billy Pierce with the '55 White Sox. Between 1963 and 1972, however, pitchers did it 21 times.

The mysterious dead ball curse finally lifted in the mid-1970s, and offensive numbers began to rise again.

JOHN PREGENZER'S FAN CLUB

In 1963, pitcher John Pregenzer was purchased by the Giants for $100 from a minor league team in Idaho. In spring training, the $100 Pregenzer fought for a spot on the roster with $150,000 bonus baby pitcher Bob Garibaldi... and made the cut! *San Francisco Chronicle* writer Novella O'Hara was intrigued and tried to buy Pregenzer from the Giants. When they turned her down, she started a fan club for him. Pregenzer became immensely popular, even before his Giants debut! Eight thousand people joined the club, including several celebrities. "One of the celebrities sent me a letter and said he couldn't join my fan club," explains Pregenzer, "and along with the letter, he sent me a hand-autographed picture, which I have hanging on my wall, and his name is John Kennedy. He was the most prestigious. He turned me down joining as a member because he said if he joined my club, he'd have to join everybody's club."

While Pregenzer's career didn't last, he had a bigger fan club than many longtime players.

LATINO PLAYERS

Latino players have been in the majors for decades, but only in the 1950s did their numbers really increase. In 1955, six Cuban-born and one Puerto Rican player debuted. Jose Valdivielso, an infielder for the Senators, was one of those players: "I was in Havana. We were playing the Nacional Union championships in Havana, and that's when Joe Cambria, who signed a lot of Cuban ballplayers in those days

Author's collection

★ **Stan Musial's last at bat, September 29, 1963, yielded hit number 3,630.**

Courtesy of Johnny Edwards

[noticed me]. He was originally from Baltimore, but he lived in Havana, and he watched baseball in Cuba for many, many years. He owned the Havana Cubans, Class B team."

In 1960, the number of new Latino players was 15, and the numbers kept increasing. In 2000, 43 Latino players debuted, most of them scouted and signed in their native countries. The foreign country that has produced the most major leaguers is the Dominican Republic, with 642 players as of 2015, followed by Venezuela with 341. The first and only all-Latino All-Star Game (AL vs. NL) was held in 1963 at the Polo Grounds.

PENNANT NOT IN CARDS FOR PHILS

FROM 1958 to 1961, the Phillies finished in last place. The '61 team's 47-107 record, which included a 23-game losing streak, was one of the worst in history. Things improved in 1962, and in '63, they finished in fourth place with a solid 87-75 record.

Things looked promising in 1964. Come September, the Phils seemed like a shoo-in for the pennant. As of September 20, they had a 6½-game lead over the Cardinals with 12 left to play. World Series tickets were printed, and the city was abuzz.

But things quickly crumbled. The Phils lost 10 in a row! Winning their final two wasn't enough, because their fate was now in the hands of others.

Bob Oldis was a catcher for the '64 Phils: "We went to St. Louis and lost three in a row to St. Louis, who took over first place. Then we went to Cincinnati, and St. Louis could have got beat the last game of the season, 'cause my buddy Al Jackson was pitching for the Mets that day. He was leading the Cardinals, and then everything was back and forth. Last game of the season and we're playing Cincinnati, and I think we put a big five or six spot up in the middle of the game, and the Cardinals were getting beat. After we put that big number up, the Cardinals came back and put a big

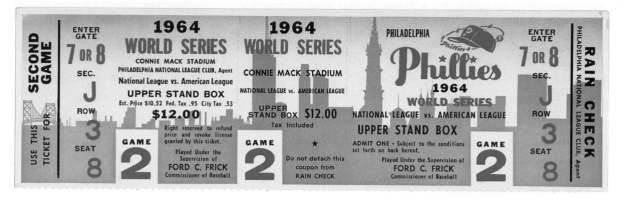

number up and beat the Mets and clinched the pennant."

They finished a game behind the Cardinals (11 games behind in late August), who went on to beat the Yankees in the World Series. Ray Sadecki, a pitcher for the Cardinals, says, "In one week, we won the pennant, I won 20 ball games, and I was starting the first game of the World Series. At 23 years of age. And that's kind of how our club went, too. Seven, eight, ten games behind, and we all just kind of put it all together."

YANKEES DECLINE

THE YANKEES' dominance ended suddenly in 1964 with their loss to the Cardinals in the World Series. Mel Stottlemyre, pitcher for the '64 Yanks, recalls, "I know the general feeling on the ball club after losing the series that year was, everybody felt, *Well, no big deal. We'll be back next year, and we'll win next year.* But that

★ **World Series tickets were printed but the Phillies didn't make it.** Author's collection

Bunt for a Hit

IT TAKES LOTS OF PRACTICE and control to avoid bunting foul or popping the ball into the air. To bunt, a player stands so he or she is facing the pitcher, brings the bat forward at about chest height, and nudges the bat so it makes soft contact with the ball, ideally sending the ball dribbling halfway into the infield. Any harder than that and the bunt is fielded like a regular ground ball. Too soft and the catcher can easily retrieve it and get an out at any base.

Most bunts these days are sacrifice bunts, with the intent of forcing an out at first to advance a runner. A successful, speedy bunter can bunt for a base hit, sometimes by pulling off a drag bunt. Usually done by left-handed hitters because they face first base, a batter begins to break for first simultaneous with the

ball hitting the bat, creating the appearance that the batter is "dragging" the ball along with him or her.

You Will Need
★ Bat
★ Softball
★ A few friends
★ Baseball field

Have a friend play the pitcher and another the first baseman. The pitcher should toss the ball to you. Try to bunt it down the first base line, and see if you can beat the throw to first. If you get to first safely score one point for yourself. Take turns so that your friends get to bunt also. Remember, three foul bunts and you're out!

Author's collection

year basically never came for a lot of years. And the majority of players that were on that ball club were older veteran players, and most of them assured me, they said, 'No big deal. We'll win next year.' It didn't happen."

The next year was very disappointing as the storied Yanks had their first losing season in 40 years. The team batting average was just .235. Roger Maris played only part of the year and hit just eight homers. Mickey Mantle hit 19. It was downhill from there as their best players continued to age, retire, or get traded. The team did not win a pennant again until 1976.

TED BOWSFIELD, 1958 RED SOX:
"Bobby Doerr and Johnny Pesky of the Red Sox, when I first came up, they told me something that resonated and stayed with me for a long time. They said, 'Look, if you learn how to bunt, and the game is 2–1, and you're in the seventh inning, and there's a runner on, the manager knows you can get that runner over. He may keep you in the ball game.' And that was absolutely true back in those days. So I became a very good bunter, to the point that I even became a very good drag bunter and got a number of my base hits by bunting."

INSIDE PITCH

WEATHER IS one of baseball's biggest foes. The first team to tackle this problem was Houston, who opened the world's first indoor, air-conditioned ball park in 1965. According to Al Spangler, a member of the original 1962 Colt .45s, "It was really awe-inspiring just to go in there for the first time. I remember when I first came down here in '62, the owner told us that, 'Two or three years, you boys are gonna be playing indoors.' And of course we all laughed behind his back, but it was quite a sight—quite a sight, but you couldn't see the ball in the outfield until they painted the dome."

Special indoor-tolerant grass was used in the Astrodome, but once the Lucite dome was painted to prevent fly balls from being lost in the light, the grass died and the rest of the 1965 season was played on painted dirt.

But a newly patented invention called Astro-Turf was on the horizon for 1966. According to Astro Ken Mackenzie, "Spring training at Coco Beach this guy drove up in a station wagon, he rolled out this green carpet. And Paul Richards came over with a fungo bat and two or three baseballs and got Claude Raymond to go down and field some balls, and I caught the balls. Claude threw it back to me, and I handed it to Paul Richards. We did that for about 10 minutes, and then he handed the bat and the ball

to me and he said to the guy, 'Try making that nap about an eighth of an inch longer.' He got in his golf cart and drove away. And that was the first AstroTurf."

> *I*n 1965, A's owner Charlie Finley, known for his wacky promotions, held "Campy Campaneris Night" in which shortstop Bert Campaneris played every position during the course of the game. When Campaneris took over catching duties in the ninth, he was knocked out in a play at the plate and missed the next five games.

★ **Astrodome interior.** Library of Congress HAER TX-108-12

> *M*any players over the years have been both Yankees and Mets. The first ex-Met to be picked up by the Yankees was Duke Carmel, who joined the club in 1965 after playing for the Mets in '63. He also played on the same team with another Duke—Duke Snider, onetime Dodger and the reason for Carmel's nickname.

This fake grass would be used in other stadiums in the years to come. Fielding on Astro-Turf could be a challenge; balls were prone to bounce over fielders' heads.

The enclosed stadium later became obsolete. It was replaced by stadiums with retractable roofs. The Astros, Seattle Mariners, Arizona Diamondbacks, and Toronto Blue Jays play in stadiums with movable roofs that can be opened and closed depending on the weather.

BASEBALL IN JAPAN

HAVING ENJOYED watching Babe Ruth, Lou Gehrig, and others on a 1934 barnstorming trip, the Japanese soon organized their own baseball teams. Interrupted by World War II, Japanese baseball made a comeback in the late 1940s. The first American to play in Japan was Wally Yonamine in 1951. More goodwill tours by teams including the Dodgers and Cardinals in the 1950s helped pave the way for the more than 600 Americans who've played in Japan since then. Most of these players headed overseas after their major league careers ended.

Cultural differences resulted in some funny scenarios. Glenn Mickens, of the 1959 Kintetsu Buffaloes, recalls one: "The manager's name was Chiba. And it was about the eighth inning, and it was hot and humid in Japan. I was out of gas, and he knew it. We were leading, and they weren't leading too many ball games. So he was sitting there at the bench trying to think of something that would stimulate me to go that one more in the ninth inning, and he says, 'Remember Pearl Harbor!' And I almost fell off the bench. Here are these Japanese telling me to remember Pearl Harbor, so I'd be mad enough to go out and beat that club."

One of the biggest American stars was former Giant Darryl Spencer, who played seven years with the Hankyu Braves, hit 142 home runs, and taught the Japanese to be more aggressive on the field.

"I did crazy things, and they liked it," says Spencer. "In a matter of a week over there [I did several things.] Playing first base I tagged a runner hard. I just reached around, you grab the ball, you reach around and tag him; I tagged him kind of hard, and he fell down. Two days later I broke up a double play sliding into second, which they had never done. We won the game 1–0. About three days later, I knocked the third baseman down, and the next night I knocked the catcher down in the bottom of the ninth to win a ball game for us. So all of a sudden our guys started sliding, and no one ever used to slide on double plays. They'd go into second base, and they'd turn out to right field about 10 feet before they got to second."

The biggest Japanese star was Sadaharu Oh, who hit 868 home runs in a 22-year career with the Yomiuri Giants. His team won the Japan Series nine straight years.

The first Japanese-born player to make the majors was Masanori Murakami in 1964. He was the only one until Hideo Nomo in 1995. Since then, more than 40 other Japanese-born players have played in the majors, including Ichiro Suzuki, who holds the single-season record for hits.

DODGERS PITCH WAY TO VICTORY

THE PENNANT-WINNING 1966 Dodgers had one of the greatest pitching rotations in history. Featuring Sandy Koufax, who had a phenomenal 27-9 season (1.73 ERA), the rotation also consisted of Don Drysdale, Don Sutton, and Claude Osteen. The foursome would end up with a combined 894 career wins. It was not only the starters who were great; the team's closer, Phil Regan, was 14-1 with a 1.62 ERA, and the overall team ERA was a league-leading 2.62.

"We didn't have very many losing streaks," says Claude Osteen about the '66 team. "Someone would stop it within those four. And that was with conditions where we really didn't have a lot of offensive might. We were very good at manufacturing runs and coming up with the run that it took to win the game. It was really good baseball. Sound baseball. You know you're not going to get many, so you don't give

★ **Dodgers program, 1966.** Author's collection

up many. And we kept our team in the game and managed to win a lot of those games in the late innings."

500 × 4

BEFORE 1965, only Babe Ruth, Mel Ott, Jimmie Foxx, and Ted Williams had reached the 500 home run plateau. Then, in the space of a few years, four sluggers who'd debuted in the early 1950s reached 500. First was Willie Mays on September 13, 1965, then Mickey Mantle on May 14, 1967; Eddie Mathews on July 4, 1967; followed by his teammate Hank Aaron on July 14, 1968. In 2007, Mantle's 500th home run ball sold at auction for $144,000.

Mantle's 1967 teammate Dooley Womack recalls number 500: "Stu Miller was in the game and he threw him one of his screwballs, and Mick picked it up, I guess, off the outside part of the plate, and pulled it out of the ballpark. And he came around the bases, of course we were all, just like all the fans and everyone, we were clapping for him, and he got to the stairs and everything, and we had padded seats, so, he jumped from the stairs and spun around and sat down and said, 'I'm glad that's over with.' And everyone was saying go out and take your curtain call, which he did." Stu Miller recalls: "Had to wait until it all died down, and then I went on and finished the game."

THE YEAR OF THE PITCHER

THE YEAR 1968 saw some incredible pitching performances. Leading the NL was the amazing Bob Gibson, whose 1.12 ERA was the lowest since 1914. Johnny Edwards, who was Gibson's catcher, recalls, "He was a fast pitcher, and we'd go over the hitters before the game, and he says, 'I don't know if I'm gonna win or lose, but the game is gonna be over in two hours.' And once the game started, if somebody didn't get in the box right away and all that stuff, hell, he'd yell at 'em, 'Get in the box!' And, boy, they knew if they didn't, they might be eating one in the ribs."

The AL had five pitchers with ERAs under 2.00, including Denny McLain of the Tigers, whose 31 victories was the most since 1931. It was also the first time that back-to-back no hitters were ever thrown by opposing teams. Gaylord Perry of the Giants threw one against the Cardinals on September 17, and then Ray Washburn came out the next day and returned the favor against the Giants.

"I didn't feel any different," says Washburn. "I just came out the next day and warmed up as usual, started the game and things just kind of keep rolling along. And you get down to the last couple of innings, then you've only got six outs, and you realize where you are."

There were other signs of the year's pitching dominance, too: the Yankees batted .214, Don

Drysdale pitched 58.2 consecutive scoreless innings, and the All-Star Game was a 1–0 NL win with a total of 20 strikeouts and just eight hits.

In 1969, in response to this low-scoring epidemic, the pitcher's mound was lowered from 15 inches to the current 10 inches in height, and the strike zone was tightened.

"It was a pitcher era," recalls Yankee Stan Bahnsen. "They lowered the mound the next year. That influenced me quite a bit. I threw over the top, and it took me a while to adjust to that. It hurt a lot of pitchers, power pitchers."

SECOND EXPANSION AND THE MIRACLE METS

THE 1969 expansion saw baseball return to Kansas City, even though the Athletics had left in 1967. It also saw the first big league team for Seattle. The Royals still exist today, but the Seattle Pilots only lasted one season before moving to Wisconsin and becoming the Brewers. "We go to spring training thinking we're going to Seattle," says Pilots catcher Jerry McNertney, "and then in spring training we find out the franchise had been sold. We're headed for Milwaukee."

In the NL, San Diego got a team called the Padres, 60 years after the minor league Padres first began playing. Montreal, which had a prominent minor league team (the Royals)

★ Ray Washburn (left) and Earl Wilson, game three starters, 1968 World Series. Courtesy of Ray Washburn

from 1897 to 1960, was awarded a major league franchise called the Expos, the first team outside of the United States.

"Our goal in '70 was to win 70," says original Expo Ron Fairly. "My God, that means we get to lose 90 games. That was our goal, win 70 in '70. We ended up winning 73. Everybody thought that was great."

It was an exciting year for New York fans because the lowly Mets made a miracle run for the pennant. In second place for much of the summer, they were unstoppable down the stretch. The Mets, who finished eight games ahead of the Cubs, won 22 games and lost only 5 at the end of the season. They beat Atlanta in the playoffs and won the World Series against Baltimore, 4–1.

SAVE IT FOR '69

CUBS CLOSER Phil Regan led the majors in saves in 1968 and didn't even know it! That's because the "save" did not exist as a statistic until 1969 when the save rule was created to credit a pitcher who enters a game and holds his team's lead; if there was more than one reliever it was up to the scorer to decide who would earn the save. Saves were calculated retroactively for pitchers in all previous seasons and added to their statistics. In 1975, the rule was changed, specifying that a pitcher had to finish a game to earn a save, and that he had to come in with a lead of no more than three runs or with the tying run at the plate or on deck (meaning that coming into a 10–6 game in the ninth with the bases loaded, he would qualify for the save).

PLAYOFFS

ONCE THE two leagues were split into two divisions each in 1969, the road to the World Series became more complicated. There were now divisional playoffs to determine who would advance, East vs. West. The joy of finishing first was now softened by the understanding that you still had another step to go.

"We had such a large lead in Cincinnati," says Ty Cline of the 1970 Reds, "I think 18 or 19 games going into the playoffs, and here you are in a two-out-of-three series. You know if you don't win two of the games, you're gone."

THE PLAYERS UNION

AFTER DECADES of limited players' rights, changes that happened in the 1960s gave players more of a say in their futures. It started with Marvin Miller, who was appointed head of the Major League Baseball Players Association in 1966.

Bob Saverine, an infielder for the Senators, remembers, "When we got into spring training with Marvin Miller, what he did was, he said, 'You don't have to tell me your name and your salary, but I'll give you a white piece of paper. If you could just put your salary on the white piece of paper, I'll have some numbers to go by.' So we all turned in our salaries to him, and he saw what we were making, and how much the owners were making, and that's how he knew that we were being taken advantage of."

Under Miller's leadership, the players' union negotiated their first collective-bargaining agreement in 1968, allowing them to have an independent arbitrator rule on grievances with club owners. In 1973, a system of salary arbitration was introduced where a player with three years of service could request an unbiased arbitrator to mediate between his salary demands and the club's.

★

THE MONEY ERA

1970–TODAY

There have been many changes to baseball since 1970. The introduction of the designated hitter rule, free agency, further expansion, skyrocketing salaries, and cable television all have had a big impact on the game. Players are stronger and faster than ever before, though allegations of steroid use have marred some players' careers.

THE END OF THE RESERVE CLAUSE

THE "RESERVE clause" tied players to their clubs. Teams pretty much owned their players and could do with them whatever they wished. Buddy Lively (1947 Reds) recalls advice his father gave him: "'Make sure you know what you're doing,' he said, 'because once you sign that contract, they can trade you for a billy goat if they want to.'"

"We were bound to the club," says 1950s pitching star Curt Simmons. "You either quit, or they could trade you or release you. They were in control."

Many players wound up floundering in the minors when major league teams wanted them. It happened to pitcher Ralph Mauriello in 1957: "The Reds offered $50,000 for my contract, and I called up Buzzie [Bavasi] and said, 'It's a profit. Sell!' They had given me a bonus of $35,000, and that was what I was alluding to.... And, you know, his response was, 'You kidding me? You're gonna be one of our starters next year.' And of course it didn't happen."

But by the late 1960s, times were ripe for change. In 1969, after a dispute over salary, the contending Cardinals sought to trade Curt Flood to the last place Phillies. He refused to go and did not report to the Phillies in 1970. His case, *Flood v. Kuhn*, went before the US Supreme Court in 1972. Though the Court ruled against Flood, the case opened the door to further questioning of the reserve clause.

In 1975, the Dodgers refused to give Andy Messersmith a no-trade clause in his contract. He pitched the season without a contract and was then deemed a free agent. In 1976, a free agency system was introduced whereby a player with six years of service in the majors who is not under contract becomes eligible to sign with any team he wishes. The days of a player as a club's property were finally over.

HUNT'S HIT

GETTING HIT by a pitch is the last thing most batters want... but not second baseman Ron Hunt. It started when he was with the Mets and overheard Gil Hodges explaining how the outside two inches of the plate belong to the pitcher. (Most batters in their normal stance have trouble making solid contact with pitches on the outside edge.) Hunt had an idea that would not only allow him to reclaim the outside of the plate but also get him free passes to first base.

"I thought, well, how about if I crowd the plate, blouse the uniform. [Then] the inside two inches is the pitcher's. The rest of the plate's mine. And if he comes in too hard, he'll hit me," Hunt recalls. "So I worked on it in front of a mirror.... And I never took my eye off the ball just in case I misread the pitch."

His strategy worked. Hunt led the league in being hit by pitches seven years in a row, including an incredible 50 times in 1971. Since 1900, nobody else has even come close to that record.

STRIKE ONE

AT THE start of the 1972 season, Marvin Miller led the union into the first-ever big league strike. Between April 1 and 13, no games were played. The strike ended when the players and owners agreed on salary and pension issues. Because of the strike, teams played anywhere from 153 to 156 games that season instead of the regular 162.

Eddie Kasko, who was the Red Sox manager that year, says: "The commissioner decided that we were gonna pick up the season right where it was and play it out just the way it was. And it turned out that we played one less game than Detroit, and they beat us by a half a game. And I never felt that was fair."

THE DESIGNATED HITTER

THE AMERICAN and National Leagues played by the same rules until 1973, when the AL adopted the designated hitter (DH) rule, which allowed teams to have a non-position player bat for the pitcher.

The rule affected the way the game is played. The pitcher was almost always in the ninth spot in the lineup, but the DH could be placed in the heart of the lineup. Managers no longer had to pinch hit for their pitchers late in the game. The pitcher could stay in and leave the job of sparking the offense to the DH. The DH rule also meant that older sluggers who couldn't run or field well anymore had a place.

What did pitchers of the time think of the rule? Opinions varied. For Yankee hurler Sam McDowell, it was a positive: "When I came from the Giants and went back to the American League with the Yankees, I personally liked sitting on the bench and just sitting and thinking about the next three or four hitters that I was going to face, instead of thinking about hitting and who the pitcher was and what his strengths and weaknesses were and the whole rigmarole that you go through."

Claude Osteen, who pitched for the White Sox in 1975, thought differently: "I had a chance to pitch in Chicago my last active year, and I just felt totally useless because there were plenty of times when I thought I could have done something about my own destiny with my bat, but you just go out there and pitch, come back in and sit down and rest, and then go out there and pitch again, and you have nothing to say about your offensive destiny."

715

Hank Aaron, one of the first great African American sluggers, didn't start out that way. His minor league teammate Johnny Goryl remembers the 1952 season: "He was the only guy I had ever seen that ever hit cross-handed, and he hit cross-handed that whole season, and he ended up hitting about .330-something, I don't know what the exact number was, but he hit the whole season cross-handed. He was a shortstop when he joined us, and next year they converted him to the outfield and showed him a conventional grip hitting, and that's when he took off as a power hitter."

For 20 straight years, Aaron hit at least 24 homers per year. After the Braves moved to Atlanta in 1966, Aaron continued to impress. By the end of the 1970 season, Aaron was approaching the 600 mark. Aaron showed no signs of slowing down, and as the end of the 1973 season approached, it seemed likely the 39-year-old slugger would reach Ruth's mark of 714 homers.

Though he had plenty of fans, Aaron also had to contend with racism as he approached the Babe's record. He received thousands of letters a week, including death threats. But the graceful Aaron didn't let it affect his on-field demeanor. He kept playing and hitting home runs. His final homer of the 1973 season, on September 29, was number 713, which meant he had to endure a long winter of anticipation—and many more letters, both supporting and opposing him.

The 1974 season opened with a three-game series in Cincinnati. The Braves wanted Aaron to sit out so he could break the record at home, but the commissioner said Aaron had to play at least two of the three against the Reds. In the first inning of the first game, with two men on, Hank Aaron came to bat and smacked number 714 to tie Ruth's record.

★ RIGHT: Hank Aaron waves to fans at the parade preceding the All-Star Game in 2008. Author's collection

Jack Billingham, the pitcher who gave up the record-tying home run, has nothing but praise for Aaron: "I remember I came in against him my second year in the big leagues, when I was a reliever with Houston. It was the 10th inning, and we were playing in Atlanta, and I walk out, and he's the first hitter. He hits a home run. We walk off the field. So I didn't get anybody out and didn't do anything but got an *L* next to my name the next day in the newspapers. But there's not any shame or embarrassment or anything else in giving up a home run to Hank Aaron. Hank Aaron is, to me, the best home run hitter in baseball. Still."

When Aaron hit number 715 four days later against the Dodgers, fireworks were set off. The new home run king moved to the Brewers in 1975 and played two years as their designated hitter. He finished his career in 1976, with a total of 755 home runs and a lifetime .305 average.

TREATING PITCHING INJURIES

IF A pitcher plays 10 years, he probably throws at least 40,000 to 50,000 pitches. That's a lot! Very few pitchers make it through their careers without an arm injury. Pitchers often played injured (with the help of cortisone shots) rather than lose their spot on the roster, adjusting their delivery or pitch selection. But pitching

Tommy John. *Author's collection*

injured can result in further injuries; playing on an injured leg puts more strain on the other leg, making it vulnerable.

Today there are treatments and surgeries available to keep players in the game. Ulnar collateral ligament (UCL) reconstruction is a common elbow surgery today, but when it was first performed in 1974, doctors gave Tommy John a 1-in-100 chance of recovery. John went on to pitch another 15 years and made it into the Hall of Fame. In 1981, Mets pitcher Craig Swan was the first to come back from a torn rotator cuff—without any surgery. "I was the first player that they didn't do the old surgery on," says Swan. "Dr. Parkes, the team physician at the time, decided not to do the old surgery, because in 1980 we didn't have arthroscopic surgery perfected for that injury yet, and nobody had recovered from the old surgery they did. And so Dr. Parkes, noting that nobody had ever come back to pitch from that surgery—'cause they had to tear everything apart to get to the rotator cuff and then repair it and then sew everything back together—he said, 'We're gonna try something new.' And I said, 'What's that?' And he said, 'We're not going to do anything.' The solution in Swan's case was a combination of rest and a therapy technique called Rolfing.

PETE ROSE AND THE BIG RED MACHINE

THE CINCINNATI Reds dominated the NL from 1970 to 1976. The "Big Red Machine" won four pennants and two World Series. Led by Johnny Bench, George Foster, and Joe Morgan, the Reds' most powerful weapon was probably Pete Rose. Nicknamed "Charlie Hustle," Rose could beat out a weak ground ball and turn it into a single. He hustled his way to 746 doubles, which is second on the all-time list, and he leads in games played, at bats, and hits. (He broke Ty Cobb's record of 4,191 in 1985.)

Billy DeMars, 1985 Phillies coach, was amazed at Rose's work ethic: "He hit every day. He never took a day off from hitting. All my days off, I spent down at the ballpark throwing to him. One night in Philadelphia, I didn't get home until one o'clock in the morning. When the game was over, he [had] said, 'Billy, I want to go down to hit.' So we went down to hit, and by the time I got home it was one o'clock. . . . I was coaching third base the night he broke Ty Cobb's hit record. I've never been around a guy

*T*oday's minimum major league salary is one hundred times higher than it was in the 1950s. Says Bobby Bolin, who pitched from 1961 to 1973, "I tell everybody I played in the BM: Before Money."

who was such a positive thinker. If he went 5-5, he was gonna go 6-6."

Unfortunately, Rose was banned from MLB for life in 1989 for gambling on games he'd managed.

RISING SALARIES

THE TOP salary in 1970 was Willie Mays at $135,000, but by 1979, Nolan Ryan became the first to reach $1 million. By 1980, the minimum was $30,000, and in 1990, it hit $100,000. In 2014, the minimum salary reached $500,000, the *average* major league salary was $3.38 million, and there were 20 players making between $20 and $30 million a year. The astronomical rise in salaries is due in part to profits teams make from lucrative broadcasting deals.

STRIKE TWO

IN 1981, a strike took place from June 12 to August 10, resulting in a split season. Teams played between 102 and 110 games that year. Division leaders from the first and second halves of the season advanced to the playoffs.

THE LONGEST GAME

THE LONGEST professional baseball game ever played began innocently enough on April 18, 1981. It was between the Rochester Red Wings and the Pawtucket Red Sox. After nine innings, the score was tied 2–2. Little could anyone imagine that the game would drag on for another 24 innings!

"It was about 38 degrees, cold, wind was blowing off the waters," remembers Doc Edwards, Red Wings manager. "That had more to do with the length of the game than anything. We couldn't hit the ball out of the ballpark. The wind was strong and it was cold. You hit a ball hard, and the wind would just beat it down."

When the seemingly endless game was stopped after the 32nd inning, at 4:09 am, there were only a handful of fans left. Once the game resumed on June 23, it took only 18 minutes for the Paw Sox to win 3–2. A total of 882 pitches were thrown, 60 strikeouts were recorded, and three players had 14 at bats in the 8 hour, 25 minute game.

CUBS END DROUGHT

AFTER NEARLY four decades without a postseason appearance, Cubs fans were ever hopeful, but their fifth place finish in the NL East in 1983 didn't bode well for the immediate future. Enter manager Jim Frey, who'd taken the Royals to the World Series in 1980. Everything came together for the '84 Cubbies, and after July 31, the team maintained a lock on first place. Though

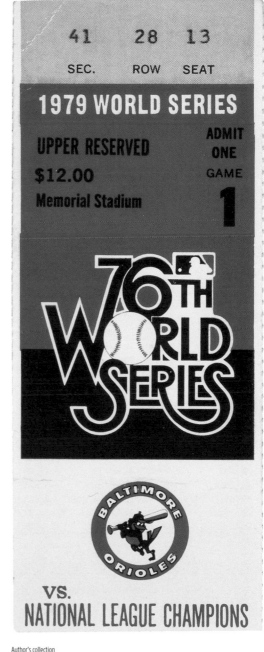

Author's collection

Gillette 1985 All-Star Game Official Ballot
Formule Officielle de Sélection des Étoiles 1985

	NATIONAL LEAGUE		AMERICAN LEAGUE	
1b	Brock	D. Green	Buckner	Hrbek
	Cabell	K. Hernandez	Carew	Mattingly
	Driessen	Rose	Cooper	E. Murray
	Durham	J. Thompson	A. Davis	O'Brien
	Garvey	Samuel	Barrett	Upshaw
2b	Doran	Sandberg	Ju. Cruz	Randolph
	Herr	S. Sax	Gantner	Teufel
	Hubbard	Trillo	D. Garcia	Whitaker
	Ray	Wiggins	Grich	F. White
SS/AC	Bowa	Reynolds	D. Concepcion	Gutierrez
	Brooks	B. Russell	T. Fernandez	S. Owen
	D. Concepcion	O. Smith	Ju. Franco	Ripken
	DeJesus	Templeton	A. Griffin	Trammell
	R. Ramirez	Madlock	B. Bell	Yount
3b	Cey	Nettles	W. Boggs	Gaetti
	Garner	Pendleton	Brett	C. Lansford
	Horner	M. Schmidt	DeCinces	Molitor
	Knight	Wallach	Da. Evans	Mulliniks
C/R	Brenly	T. Pena	Boone	Heath
	G. Carter	D. Porter	Dempsey	Lan. Parrish
	J. Davis	Scioscia	Fisk	Sundberg
	Fitzgerald	Virgil	Gedman	Whitt
	Kennedy	Matthews	Armas	Wynegar
Outfield/ Voltigeur	J. Clark	McGee	Baines	Kittle
	Jo. Cruz	McReynolds	Barfield	Lacy
	C. Davis	Moreland	Baylor (DH)	Lemon
	Dawson	Mumphrey	G. Bell	Lynn
	Dernier	Da. Murphy	Brunansky	Moseby
	Foster	Parker	Butler	Dw. Murphy
	Guerrero	Puhl	Collins	Oglivie
	Gwynn	Raines	Downing	Lar. Parrish
	Hayes	L. Smith	Easler (DH)	Puckett
	Hendrick	Strawberry	Dw. Evans	Rice
	Kemp	C. Washington	K. Gibson	Ward
	J. Leonard	M. Wilson	R. Henderson	W. Wilson
	Marshall	Wynne	Re. Jackson	Winfield

PRINTED IN U.S.A.

Perforez ce rectangle seulement si vous inscrivez un autre choix au bas. Punch out only if you write in your vote.

Pos.	Player/Joueur	Pos.	Player/Joueur

Please send my refund for Atra Razor / Foamy Smooth / Right Guard to:
Veuillez m'envoyer un remboursement pour rasoir
Atra / Foamy Formule Douce / Désodorisant en bâton Right Guard à:

Name/Nom: _____
Address/Adresse: _____
City/Ville: _____ Province: _____ Postal Code/Code Postal: _____

Additional terms: This certificate must accompany your request and may not be reproduced. Offer expires July 31, 1985. Only one certificate per household. Allow 6-8 weeks for delivery.
Conditions supplémentaires: Ce certificat doit accompagner votre demande et ne doit pas être reproduit. L'offre se termine le 31 juillet, 1985. Un seul certificat par adresse. Accordez de 6 à 8 semaines pour la livraison.

★ **1985 All-Star ballot.** Author's collection

---

they would later lose to the Padres in the NL Championship Series, Frey received the Manager of the Year Award and Cubs fans finally had a season to remember.

"When I got to Chicago during the winter for a visit," recalls Frey, "somebody said to me, 'You know our history here. After Labor Day, if you get to the park late, you have to sit in the second row.' So I remembered that remark, and we got on a roll there after we beat the Mets those two series, and we kinda stayed there.... I remember distinctly standing in the dugout with a pitching coach by the name of Billy Connors, and he said to me at one point in the early or middle part of September, he said, 'We've got 37,000, and 1,500 standing room only,' and they hadn't experienced that in I don't know how many years, so that was a big thrill."

THE '86 METS

AFTER TWO years of second place finishes, the 1986 Mets were ready to make a move. They were scrappy, brash, and even arrogant—but very talented. Led by the young phenom Dwight Gooden, the starting rotation had an incredible

76-30 record. At 108-54, the Mets won the NL East by 21½ games.

The '86 World Series against the Red Sox featured one of the most infamous errors in baseball history. In game six, Boston first baseman Bill Buckner let a Mookie Wilson ground ball go through his legs in the bottom of the 10th inning. The error allowed the winning run to score. The Mets went on to win game seven and take the series.

The '86 Mets remain one of the most legendary teams in baseball history. Doug Sisk was a relief pitcher on the team: "When you get in your little world when you're playing the game, you forget all the people that are watching this and how important it is to all these people, this game. But we're down there playing it, 'cause we have the natural God-given ability to play this game. And only when we retire and get out of the game do we look back and go, *Holy Cow, how the heck did I do it?*"

STRIKE THREE!

ON AUGUST 12, 1994, a disagreement between the players and owners resulted in the players being locked out. The rest of the season was canceled, and for the first time, the World Series was not played. Fans were upset and disenchanted. Instead of a rush back to the ballparks when play resumed in 1995, attendance fell.

MORE EXPANSION

BASEBALL CONTINUED to expand its reach in the 1970s with the addition of the Seattle Mariners and Toronto Blue Jays. The Florida Marlins and Colorado Rockies debuted in 1993. The Marlins finished in sixth place their first year, but by 1997, they were World Series champions. After a couple of years in last place, in 2003 72-year-old Jack McKeon led them to another championship, becoming the oldest manager ever to win a World Series.

"I was managing the Reds in 2000," explains McKeon, "and we went down to play the Marlins, and I was sitting in the dugout and watched the Marlins as they came across the field, and I said to my pitching coach, Don Gullett, 'Boy, would I love to manage that team. They've got a lot of talent over there, but they look like they're staying in neutral. Someone needs to give 'em a kick and get them up to the next level.' And two and a half years later, here I am."

The Rockies struggled at first but finally reached the World Series in 2007. In 1994, the structure of each league's divisions was changed; a Central division was added to the existing East and West divisions. The three division champs in each league were joined by a wild card team, and the playoffs became a two-step process, pushing the World Series, originally held in late September, toward the end of October. The 1998 expansion saw the addition of the Arizona Diamondbacks (2001 World Series champions) and the Tampa Bay Devil Rays, who didn't fare very well their first few years.

THE NEW IRON MAN

NOBODY THOUGHT that Lou Gehrig's consecutive-games-played record of 2,130 would ever fall. Then along came Cal Ripken Jr., son of Orioles scout, coach, and manager Cal Ripken.

Young Ripken, drafted by the Orioles at age 18, was not only an excellent infielder, he had power. He hit 431 homers and was selected as an All-Star 19 times during his 21-year career. Orioles scout Tommy Giordano remembers Cal Sr. throwing batting practice to Cal Jr.: "He was hitting line drive bleacher home runs into the left field bleachers when he was 15 or 16 years old."

Ripken was also incredibly durable for a middle infielder; on September 6, 1995, he played his 2,131st consecutive game, breaking Gehrig's 56-year-old record. Ripken voluntarily ended his streak at 2,632 games in 1998. He played another three years, retiring in 2001.

BASEBALL RETURNS TO DC

AFTER A 33-year absence, baseball returned to DC in 1995 when the Montreal Expos moved

★ **Cal Ripken's last game.** Courtesy of Beth Tenser

★ **President Obama throws out the first pitch on Opening Day in Washington, DC, 2009.** Courtesy of the Department of Defense

to Washington and became the Nationals. Five of their first six years, the Nats finished in last place. Powered by new talent such as outfielder Bryce Harper and pitcher Stephen Strasburg, along with outfielder Jayson Werth, they finished third in 2011. In 2012 they had the best record in baseball, clinching a playoff spot. It was the first time a Washington team finished in first place since 1933.

YANKEES ON TOP AGAIN

AFTER AN 11-year stretch of mostly mediocre seasons starting in 1965, the Yankees had a streak of success again that started in the mid-1970s. Powered by Reggie Jackson, the popular slugger known as "Mr. October" for his post-season home run heroics, between 1976 and 1981, the Yankees finished in first place five times and won the World Series twice.

A 12-year dry period followed, but then the Yankees surged once again. Between 1996 and 2003, the Yankees appeared in six World Series, winning five of them, including the Subway Series with the Mets in 2000.

The Yankees' success landed them in the postseason for an incredible 13 years in a row (1995–2007), led by skipper Joe Torre. Key players were fan favorites: shortstop Derek Jeter and closer Mariano Rivera, who accumulated 652 saves in 19 years with the Yanks.

GOODBYE, OLD STADIUMS

OVER THE years, most of the older ballparks have been demolished, including Ebbets Field in 1960, the Polo Grounds in 1964, Forbes Field in 1971, and Municipal Stadium in 1996. More recent losses include Yankee Stadium and Shea Stadium, both in 2008.

The replacement stadiums were designed to be more fan friendly and have more modern conveniences. Because of the high cost of building new stadiums, many of them are now named after their sponsors, such as Citi Field, AT&T Park, Coors Field, Minute Maid Park, and Petco Field.

HOME RUN RECORDS FALL

IN THE years following Roger Maris's home run barrage of 1961, the closest anyone came to breaking the record was Ken Griffey, with 56 homers in 1997. No one could have predicted that the very next year would see not one but two players break the record!

By the end of June 1998, National Leaguers Mark McGwire (Cardinals) and Sammy Sosa (Cubs) were already on a hot pace—Sosa had 33 home runs and McGwire had 37. The race continued to heat up, and by the end of August, McGwire and Sosa were tied at 55 home runs apiece. It seemed a certainty that Maris's record would fall. On September 7, McGwire tied the record, and the next day, he broke it with number 62. Sosa tied and broke Maris's record on the same day, September 13.

The next question was Who would end up with the new record? Sosa hit 11 homers in September, winding up with 66 and McGwire hit 15, for a total of 70. But just three years later, in 2001, that new record would fall when Barry Bonds slugged 73 homers.

Bonds would return to the spotlight in 2007 when he broke Hank Aaron's career home run record of 755. Bonds ended the season, and his career, with a total of 762 homers, the new record.

STEROID USE

THOUGH THE summer of 1998 was an exciting time for baseball fans, the whole thing would later be tainted, as Mark McGwire and Sammy Sosa, as well as Barry Bonds, were dogged by allegations of steroid use.

Athletes first began to use steroids or hormones to enhance their performance during the 1990s, making their muscles bigger and their bodies stronger. These advantages gave the batters greater home run power. The MLB began to crack down on steroid use in 2005. Admissions by some former baseball stars have placed a cloud over many dominant players of

Baseball Nicknames

BASEBALL PLAYERS have always been known for their amusing and colorful nicknames. Some coined their own names; others were given their names by friends, teammates, fans, or the press. Player nicknames sometimes became their official names, such as "Dizzy" Dean, but usually the nicknames complemented their real names; Ted Williams was nicknamed the "Splendid Splinter."

When Rudy Minarcin was asked his nickname in spring training, he came up with "Buster" though his childhood nickname was actually *Zemok* ("potato" in Slovakian). Charlie Maxwell is listed as "Smoky," which was mostly his nickname in high school not in his professional career. Bob Speake has no idea how he got stuck with "Spook," nor does bonus baby Tom Qualters remember anyone actually calling him "Money Bags."

When Everett Lamar Bridges was with the Greenville Spinners in 1948, his teammates said, "That's no name for a ballplayer," and called him "Rocky." Reliever Phil Regan was called "Vulture" once by fellow Dodger Sandy Koufax, and a reporter overheard it.

You Will Need
★ Pack of index cards
★ Pencils

What nicknames might fit your personality? Gather a group of friends. Count how many of you there are, and multiply by five. Hand out that many cards to each person. Each person should anonymously come up with five possible nicknames for everyone present (write the recipient of the name on top of each card), including themselves. These can be made-up names, or you can use actual baseball player nicknames. Collect the cards, shuffle them up, and read them out loud. See which name suits each of your friends best!

the 1990s and 2000s, who may never get into the Hall of Fame despite breaking all kinds of records.

On August 5, 2013, 13 players were suspended for using performance-enhancing drugs, including three time MVP Alex Rodriguez, who received a one-year suspension without pay.

★ BASEBALL NICKNAMES ★ ★ ★ ★ ★ ★ ★ ★ ★ ★ ★ ★ ★ ★ ★ ★

THE STORIES BEHIND how some baseball players got their nicknames are often stranger than the names themselves:

Turk Lown: "My first year in pro ball, I wasn't making a lot of money. And the restaurant where we ate all the time—the biggest meal on the menu was turkey. So every day I'd eat turkey, and finally the fellows started calling me Turk. And that's how I got the name."

Skeeter Kell: "The night I was born, the doctor was up at a Skeeter Kell vaudeville show [he traveled several states with the show]. My dad walked up to the show to get the doctor to come to our house to deliver me—thus, he [the doctor] named me Skeeter."

Roy Sievers: "At basketball practice, one guy said, 'You know what? You're squirrely.' So I go, 'What?' He said, 'You're squirrely.' So I come out the next day, he says, 'Hey, Squirrel, how's everything going?' My nickname just stayed with me after that. Everybody called me Squirrel after that."

INSTANT REPLAY

BEGINNING IN 2008, umpires could review video of questionable home runs—fair or foul?—in order to make a proper call. The 2014 season took instant replay even further and paved the way for one of the biggest changes in the history of the game. Managers are now allowed to challenge one call during the course of a game—except for balls and strikes. If that call is overturned, they get a second challenge to use later in the game.

Umpire crew chiefs can review video of home runs as well as collisions at home plate in order to make a proper call. After the seventh inning, they can also review any play as they see fit. There were a total of 1,265 challenged calls during the 2014 season; 48 percent were overturned.

★

YOU NEVER KNOW

Baseball has changed a lot over the course of the last century. Everything from rules, to ballparks, to salaries, to the sheer strength of the players has changed. But one thing will never change: baseball is a fascinatingly complex and exciting sport.

Anything can happen in baseball, at any time. Baseball dreams can come true, and baseball miracles can happen. Fortunes can change overnight, or from one minute to the next. One pitch, one inch, can make all the difference. As Yogi Berra famously said, "It ain't over 'til it's over." Baseball is a combination of physical, mental, and old-fashioned luck.

Ace pitcher Billy Pierce tells the story of his spring in 1962, which was toward the end of his 18-year career: "In spring training, I had an earned run average of 16.00. Everything I threw, the batters hit. I don't care who was up there, I could have rolled it, they'd hit a line drive somewhere. But it's just one of those things. It so happened that Alvin Dark had confidence in me. The last game of spring training we were losing 2–1, I think it was. They had got a couple of runs in the bottom of the inning before he said, 'I want you to pitch the ninth inning.' I did. I faced the eighth hitter, the ninth hitter, and the first hitter. I'll never forget that. And I happened to get them out. First time! They probably hit the ball hard, I don't know, but I got them out. And he said, 'Bill, we're gonna play in St. Louis the first two games, and we're going back home. You're opening up against Cincinnati.' And after a 16.00 ERA in spring training, I won the first eight games in a row. You never know."

What does the future hold for baseball?

You never know, but whatever it is, it'll sure be interesting.

ACKNOWLEDGMENTS

Thanks to all those who cheered me on and shared in my triumphs as I wrote this book. Special thanks goes out to the players who sent me photos and articles about their careers: Dick Brodowski, Johnny Edwards, Alex George, Joe Hicks, Marty Kutyna, Ed Mayer, John Pyecha, and Ray Washburn; and to Bobby Doerr for the autographed baseball card, which sat on my desk and inspired me as I wrote.

Heartfelt thanks to all the players and managers who agreed to speak with me or who wrote me and answered my questions: Tom Acker, Dick Adams, Red Adams, Bob Addis, Pat Ahearne, Gair Allie, George Altman, Joe Altobelli, Joey Amalfitano, Rugger Ardizoia, Bob Aspromonte, Ken Aspromonte, Joe Astroth, Earl Averill, Joe Azcue, Stan Bahnsen, Steve Balboni, Ray Barker, Bruce Barmes, Vic Barnhart, Dick Barone, Cuno Barragan, Tony Bartirome, Boyd Bartley, Eddie Basinski, Matt Batts, Frank Baumann, John Baumgartner, Zeke Bella, Vern Benson, Neil Berry, Fred Besana, Jack Billingham, Maybelle Blair, Bob Blaylock, Gary Blaylock, Dick Bokelmann, Jim Bolger, Bobby Bolin, Frank Bolling, Bob Borkowski, Jim Bouton, Bob Bowman, Ted Bowsfield, Cloyd Boyer, Jim Brady, Ralph Branca, Jackie Brandt, Ed Bressoud, Tom Brewer, Rocky Bridges, Lou Brissie, Dick Brodowski, Ernie Broglio, Hal Brown, Bobby Brown, Alton Brown, Cal Browning, Mack Burk, Leo Burke, George Burpo, Dick Burwell, Putsy Caballero, Fred Caligiuri, Doug Camilli, Duke Carmel, Eddie Carnett, Tom Carroll, Jerry Casale, Foster Castleman, Wayne Causey, Bob Cerv, Joe Christopher, Chuck Churn, Galen Cisco, Mel Clark, Phil Clark, Doug Clemens, Tex Clevenger, Ty Cline, Gil Coan, Jim Coates, Hy Cohen, Rocky Colavito, Dick Cole, Jerry Coleman, Jim Command, Clint Conatser, Gene Conley, Chuck Cottier, Roger Craig, Del Crandall, Jack Crimian, Ray Crone, Joe Cunningham, Angelo Dagres, Bud Daley, Pete Daley, Clay Dalrymple, Bennie Daniels, Alvin Dark, Jim Davenport, Cot Deal, Bobby Del Greco, Billy DeMars, John DeMerit, Don Demeter, Jim Derrington, Ducky Detweiler, Chuck Diering, Roy Dietzel, Art Ditmar, Tom Donohue, Whammy Douglas, Bob

Duliba, Grant Dunlap, Joe Durham, Bobby Durnbaugh, Carl Duser, Doc Edwards, Johnny Edwards, George Elder, Dick Ellsworth, Bill Endicott, Eddie Erautt, Frank Ernaga, Carl Erskine, Larry Eschen, Chuck Essegian, Chuck Estrada, Roy Face, Ron Fairly, Jack Faszholz, Chico Fernandez, Don Ferrarese, Dave Boo Ferriss, Mike Fiore, Maurice Fisher, Eddie Fisher, Ed Fitz Gerald, Tom Flanigan, Hank Foiles, Terry Fox, Paul Foytack, Tito Francona, George Freese, Jim Frey, Bob Friend, Bruce Froemming, Len Gabrielson, Joe Garagiola, Dave Garcia, Billy Gardner, Ned Garver, George Genovese, Jim Gentile, Alex George, Dick Gernert, Jake Gibbs, Bob Giggie, Buddy Gilbert, Tommy Giordano, Fred Gladding, Jim Golden, Charlie Gorin, Johnny Goryl, Alex Grammas, Lou Grasmick, Don Grate, Johnny Gray, Eli Grba, Bill Greason, Jim Greengrass, Eddie Haas, Dick Hall, Ken Hamlin, Ron Hansen, Carroll Hardy, Chuck Harmon, Billy Harrell, Bob Harrison, Jack Harshman, Don Hasenmayer, Ray Hathaway, Grady Hatton, Chris Haughey, Roy Hawes, Val Heim, Russ Heman, Solly Hemus, Gail Henley, Bobby Henrich, Bill Henry, Ray Herbert, Neal Hertweck, Johnny Hetki, Jim Hickman, Buddy Hicks, Joe Hicks, Dave Hillman, Paul Hinrichs, Jay Hook, Hal Hudson, Ron Hunt, Billy Hunter, Willard Hunter, Dick Hyde, Al Jackson, Randy Jackson, Roosevelt Jackson, Johnny James, Virgil Jester, Jim Bailey, Don Johnson, Ken Johnson, Footer Johnson, Rocky Johnson, Howie Judson, Jim Kaat, Don Kaiser, Eddie Kasko, Ted Kazanski, Skeeter Kell, Bob Kelly, Russ Kemmerer, Art Kenney, Marty Keough, Evans Killeen, Jerry Kindall, Fred Kipp, Willie Kirkland, Joe Kirrene, Bobby Knoop, Dick Koecher, Steven Korchek, Bill Koski, Steven Kraly, Chuck Kress, Rocky Krsnich, Marty Kutyna, Bob Kuzava, Jim Landis, Hobie Landrith, Joe Landrum, Don Larsen, Frank Lary, Don Lasetter, Vern Law, Don Lee, Mike Lee, Gene Leek, Jim Lefebvre, Don Lenhardt, Ted Lepcio, Don E. Leppert, Don G. Leppert, George Lerchen, Walt Linden, Charlie Lindstrom, Angelo LiPetri, Buddy Lively, Chuck Locke, Johnny Logan, Jim Lonborg, Stan Lopata, Hector Lopez, Turk Lown, Frank Lucchesi, Jerry Lumpe, Don Lund, Eric MacKenzie, Ken Mackenzie, Jim Mahoney, Bobby Malkmus, Jim Maloney, Felix Mantilla, Dick Manville, Joe Margoneri, Fred Marolewski, Jim Marshall, J. C. Martin, Bob Martyn, Gordie Massa, Len Matarazzo, Carl Mathias, Ralph Mauriello, Charlie Maxwell, Ed Mayer, Jim McAnany, Ken McBride, Lindy McDaniel, Sam McDowell, Pat McGlothin, Rogers McKee, Jack McKeon, Jack McMahan, Jim McManus, John McNamara, Jerry McNertney, Charlie Mead, Lennie Merullo, Mickey Micelotta, Ed Mickelson, Glenn Mickens, Ed Mierkowicz, Larry Miggins, Carl Miles, Bob G. Miller, Bob J. Miller, Stu Miller, Rudy Minarcin,

Don Minnick, Bill Monbouquette, Alex Monchak, Zach Monroe, Billy Moran, Bobby Morgan, Guy Morton, Don Mossi, Moon Mullen, Steven Nagy, Al Naples, Hal Naragon, Peter Naton, Ron Necciai, Cal Neeman, Ron Negray, Al Neiger, Mel Nelson, Dave Nicholson, Irv Noren, Eddie O'Brien, Johnny O'Brien, Billy O'Dell, Jim O'Rourke, Jim O'Toole, John Oldham, Bob Oldis, Claude Osteen, Bill Oster, Jim Owens, Milt Pappas, Tom Patton, Don Pavletich, Stan Pawloski, Laurin Pepper, Harry Perkowski, Ron Perranoski, Jim Perry, Gary Peters, Paul Pettit, Lee Pfund, Taylor Phillips, Billy Pierce, Jim Piersall, Rance Pless, Herb Plews, J. W. Porter, Leo Posada, John Pregenzer, Joe Presko, Buddy Pritchard, Jim Proctor, John Pyecha, Tom Qualters, Charlie Rabe, Hal Raether, Vern Rapp, Curt Raydon, Rudy Regalado, Phil Regan, Bill Renna, Fred Richards, Bobby Richardson, Pete Richert, Al Richter, Jim Rivera, Mel Roach, Mike Roarke, Don Robertson, Eddie Robinson, Ed Roebuck, Johnny Romano, Phil Roof, Al Rosen, Bob Ross, Johnny Rutherford, Ray Sadecki, Eddie Samcoff, Mike Sandlock, Frank Saucier, Bob Savage, Bob Saverine, Moe Savransky, Hal Schacker, Joe Schaffernoth, Art Schallock, Carl Scheib, Freddy Schmidt, Dick Schofield, Jerry Schoonmaker, Paul Schramka, Art Schult, Don Schwall, Jerry Schypinski, Kal Segrist, Ray Semproch, Bobby Shantz, Rollie Sheldon, Neill Sheridan, Norm Sherry, Garland Shifflett, Bill Short, George Shuba, Roy Sievers, Charlie Silvera, Curt Simmons, Duke Simpson, Doug Sisk, Dave Skaugstad, Bob Skinner, Lou Sleater, Earl Smith, Hal Smith, Paul Smith, Jerry Snyder, Jim Snyder, Al Spangler, Bob Speake, George Spencer, Darryl Spencer, Jack Spring, Joe Stanka, Dick Starr, Bob Stephenson, Chuck Stevens, Julia Ruth Stevens, Dick Stigman, Wes Stock, Dean Stone, Mel Stottlemyre, Hal Stowe, Paul Stuffel, Jim Stump, Frank Sullivan, Gordie Sundin, Craig Swan, Red Swanson, Bob Talbot, Willie Tasby, Don Taussig, Dick Teed, Ralph Terry, Wayne Terwilliger, Bert Thiel, Frank Thomas, Carolyn Thomas, Bud Thomas, George Thomas, Tim Thompson, Dick Tomanek, Frank Torre, Dick Tracewski, Bill Tremel, Bob Usher, Jose Valdivielso, Fred Valentine, Ozzie Van Brabant, Fred Van Dusen, Coot Veal, Gene Verble, Bill Virdon, Gale Wade, Jerry Walker, Ray Washburn, Neal Watlington, Ray Webster, Milt Welch, Dick Welteroth, Wally Westlake, Bill White, Ted Wieand, Bob Wiesler, Stan Williams, Jim Willis, Ted Wills, Red Wilson, Ed Winceniak, Gordie Windhorn, Bobby Winkles, Dooley Womack, Wilbur Wood, Jim Woods, Hank Workman, Al Worthington, Tom Wright, Roy Wright, George Yankowski, Tom Yewcic, Eddie Yost, Bob Zick, and George Zuverink.

RESOURCES

BOOKS

Buckley, James. *Baseball*. New York: DK Eyewitness Books, 2010.

Jacobs, Greg. *The Everything Kids' Baseball Book*. Avon, MA: Adams Media, 2014.

Le Boutillier, Nate. *The Best of Everything Baseball Book*. North Mankato, MN: Capstone Press, 2011.

Schlossberg, Dan. *The New Baseball Catalog*. Flushing, NY: Jonathan David Publishers, 1998.

Sports Illustrated Kids' Full Count: Top 10 Lists of Everything in Baseball. NY: Sports Illustrated, 2012.

WEBSITES

Baseball Statistics
www.baseballreference.com
www.baseball-almanac.com
www.retrosheet.org
Current Teams
mlb.mlb.com
www.milb.com

Images
www.loc.gov/rr/program/bib/baseball/web.html

INDEX

Teams are alphabetized under the names of their cities or states. Page numbers in italics indicate illustrations.

Schmidt, Freddy, 50

Schramka, Paul, 33, 73

Schult, Art, 64

Schwall, Don, 14

Score, Herb, 19

scoring games, 27

scouts, 2, 5, 11, 21, 53, 85 127

Seattle Mariners, 112, 127

Seattle Pilots, ix, 115

Seattle Rainiers, 37

Seaver, Tom, 107

segregation. *See* racial segregation

semipro teams, 4

Sewell, Joe, 28

Shannon, Joe, 74

Shannon, Red, 74

Shantz, Bobby, 45, 78, 83, 100

    Gold Glove awards, 85

    MVP award, 14

Shea Stadium, 128

Sheldon, Rollie, 100

Sheridan, Neill, 73, 73

Sherry, Norm, 98

Sievers, Roy, 66, 130

signs, 12, 73–74

Silvera, Charlie, 82

Simmons, Curt, 53, 120

Sisk, Doug, 126

Sisler, George, 42

Skinner, Bob, 10, 96–97

Slaughter, Enos, 18

Sleater, Lou, 69, 72

sliding, 19, 112

    and Ty Cobb, 29

slugging average calculation, 7

Smith, Hal, 91

Snider, Duke, 75, 112

Sosa, Sammy, ix, 128, 129

South Bend Blue Sox, 52

Southern Association, 51

Southworth, Billy, 9, 50

Spalding, A. J., xii, 5

Spangler, Al, 111

Speake, Bob, 2, 129

Spencer, Darryl, 45, 85, 112

Spencer, George, 5, 68

"Splendid Splinter" (Ted Williams), 43

spring training, 5–7, 6, 102

    in Arizona, 6, 79

    in Florida, 6, 55, 58

    and interleague play, 24

Springfield Sallies, 52

stadiums, 44–47

    covered, 111–112

    replacement of, 128

    See also individual teams

Staley, Gerry, 18

stealing. *See* base stealing

Stengel, Casey, 3, 12, 34–35, 45, 97, 100–102

"Stengelese," 65

Stephani, Frederick, 84

Stephenson, Bob, 18

steroids, 129

Stevens, Julia Ruth, 31, 39, 51, 59, 104

Stirnweiss, George Henry "Snuffy," 82

stolen bases. *See* base stealing

Stone, Dean, 20, 75

Stottlemyre, Mel, 12, 109

Stowe, Hal, 8

Strasburg, Stephen, 128

strikes, players', 121, 125, 126

strikeout records, 70

Sullivan, Ed, 8

Sundin, Gordie, 8, 16

Sutton, Don, 113

Suzuki, Ichiro, 113

Swan, Craig, xi, 124

switch hitters, 106

★ T

Talbot, Bob, 19, 37

Tampa Bay Devil Rays, ix, 127

Tappe, Elvin, 99

Taylor, Zack, 66

Teed, Dick, 16

Terry, Billy, 43

Terry, Ralph, 83, 97

Terwilliger, Wayne, 68

Texas League, 58

Texas Rangers, 77

    See also Washington Senators (second team)

Thayer, Ernest L., 25

Thiel, Bert, 59

Thomas, Bud, 53, 65, 92

Thomas, Frank, 47, 100

Thompson, Hank, 58

Thompson, Tim, 1

Topps baseball cards, 60, 60

Toronto Blue Jays, 112, 127

Torre, Frank, 31

Torre, Joe, 128

trades, 14, 76, 83, 90–93, 101

    and reserve clause, 120

travel, 5, 7, 18, 37

Triandos, Gus, 5

triple crown of batting, 10

triples, 25, 37

"Trolley" Series, St. Louis, 50

Trucks, Virgil, 31, 74–75

★ U

umpires, 30, 82, 98

    and video replay, 130

Usher, Bob, 33